AIRFRAME & POWERPLANT MECHANICS

GENERAL WORKBOOK

Written, Oral, and Practical

ALIGNS WITH

FAA-H-8083-30B & FAA-H-8083-30B-ATB

Airframe & Powerplant Mechanics General Handbook

by Thomas Wild and Michael Leasure

Aircraft Technical Book Company

72413 US Hwy 40 - Tabernash, CO 80478-0270 USA

(970) 726-5111

www.actechbooks.com

 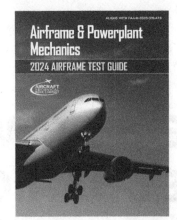 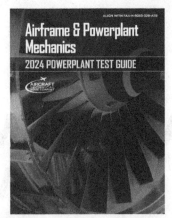

PREFACE

This Student Workbook is designed as a companion to the Aviation Maintenance Mechanics General Handbook FAA-H-8083-30B and FAA-H-8083-30B-ATB. Each chapter of this workbook matches the equivalent chapter in the Handbook and contains study questions, exercises, and a final exam for that chapter. Each is designed to enhance your understanding of the material in the textbook and to better prepare you for success with your actual FAA written exams and later in your career as a professional aviation maintenance technician.

Each chapter of this Workbook is presented in 3 parts:
1. Study Aid Questions are fill in the blank, multiple choice, true or false, or matching formats designed to reinforce the most important concepts presented in the Handbook.
2. Knowledge Application Questions; giving you an opportunity to actually use the material presented in each chapter to solve common problems.
3. Final Chapter Exam, in multiple choice format designed to further reinforce your study skills and to be used by instructors as end of chapter exam and as an evaluation of your progress.

The answers to Sections A&B questions may be found in the back of this workbook and can so be used by students as a part of your personal study habits. The answers to Section C - Final Chapter Exams, are available only to instructors as part of the instructor support package for the H-8083 textbook series, thus preserving the value of the exam as a valid instructional tool.

Each page in this book is perforated allowing students to tear out and turn in assigned sections which may be given as homework or in-class exercises.

For further information about this Workbook, its corresponding Textbook, or to order additional copies in print or electronic format, please contact Aircraft Technical Book Company at (970) 726-5111, or email to orders@actechbooks.com, or visit our web site at www.actechbooks.com.

TABLE OF CONTENTS

ISBN: 978-1951275792

Section A
Study Aid Questions - Fill In The Blanks

1. Keeping hangars, shop, and the flight-line _____ and _____ is essential to safety and efficient maintenance.

2. _____ and _____ should watch for their own safety and for the safety of others working around them.

3. Three pieces of protective safety gear which should always be used when working around electricity are: _____, _____, and _____.

4. Anytime current flows, a byproduct of that flow is _____.

5. Ensure that all power cords, wires, and lines are free of _____ and _____ which can damage the wire.

6. When inflating tires on any type of aircraft wheels, _____ should always be used.

7. _____ are very important to shop safety and making shop personnel aware of safety risks of certain materials.

8. The _____ are a more detailed version of the chemical safety issues.

9. The National Fire Protection Association (NFPA), for commercial purposes, has classified fires into three basic types: _____, _____, and _____.

10. When using _____, make sure you have the correct type for the fire.

11. _____ is any damage caused by any loose object to aircraft, personnel, or equipment.

12. When approaching a helicopter while the blades are turning, observe the rotor-head and blades to see if they are _____.

13. Before starting an aircraft engine make sure that no property damage or personal injury will occur from the _____ or _____.

14. While touching a _____, always assume that the ignition is on.

15. Unlike _____ engine aircraft, the turbojet-powered aircraft does not require a preflight run-up unless it is necessary to investigate a suspected malfunction.

SAFETY, GROUND OPERATIONS, AND SERVICING

Section A
True or False

_____ 1. Human factors should be introduced to aircraft maintenance personnel to make them aware of how it affects the maintenance performed.

_____ 2. Maintenance technicians need not be aware of how human factors can affect their performance and safety while performing maintenance practices.

_____ 3. Keeping hangars, shop, and flight-lines orderly and clean is essential to safety and efficient maintenance.

_____ 4. Safety lanes, walkways, or fire lanes should not be painted around the perimeter inside hangars.

_____ 5. To safely deal with electricity, the technician must have a working knowledge of the principles of electricity, and a healthy respect for its capability to do both work and damage.

_____ 6. Two factors that affect safety with electricity are, dampness and how much electricity you can stand.

_____ 7. Anytime current flows, whether during generation or transmission, a byproduct of that flow is heat.

_____ 8. Compressed air, like electricity, is an excellent tool as long as it is under control.

_____ 9. Using compressed air to clean hands or clothing can force debris into the flesh leading to infection.

_____ 10. The most observable portion of the MSDS Label is the risk diamond; a 4 color segmented diamond that represents Flammability (Red), Reactivity (Yellow), Health (Blue) and special Hazard (White).

_____ 11. In the Flammability, Reactivity, and Health blocks there should be a number from 0 to 2.

_____ 12. Hazards in a shop's operation increase when the operation of lathes, drill presses, grinders, and other types of machines are used.

_____ 13. Since most petroleum products float on water, water-type fire extinguishers are very much recommended for Class B fires.

_____ 14. Never use water-type fire extinguishers on Class D fires. Because metals burn at extremely high temperatures, the cooling effect of water causes an explosive expansion of the metal.

_____ 15. When performing maintenance on the flight-line you must always be aware of what is going on around you.

SAFETY, GROUND OPERATIONS, AND SERVICING

Section B
Knowledge Application Questions

Fill In The Blanks: Identify these standard FAA hand taxi signals below.

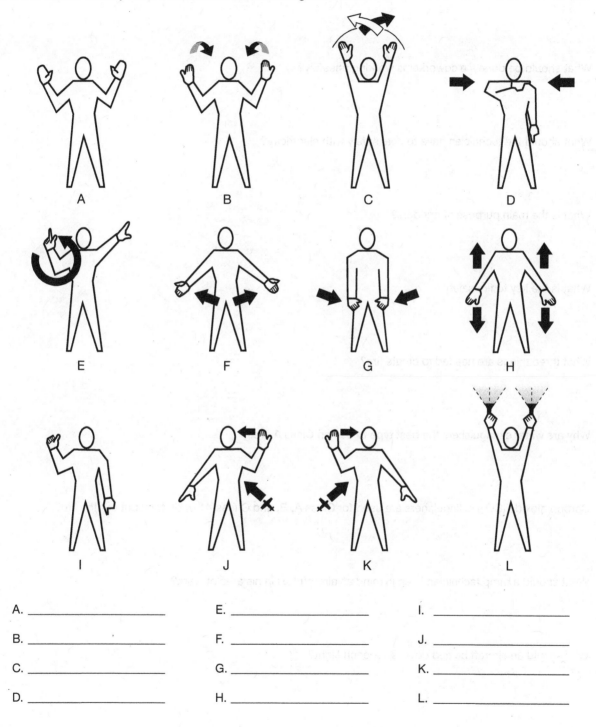

A. _____

B. _____

C. _____

D. _____

E. _____

F. _____

G. _____

H. _____

I. _____

J. _____

K. _____

L. _____

SAFETY, GROUND OPERATIONS, AND SERVICING

Section B
Short Answers

1. Why should human factors be introduced to aircraft maintenance personnel?

2. What should be done if a coworker is working unsafely?

3. What should the technician have to deal safely with electricity?

4. What is the main purpose of grinders?

5. What is the key to fire safety?

6. What three things are needed to create fire?

7. Why are water extinguishers the best type to use on Class A fires?

8. Carbon dioxide (CO_2) extinguishers are used for Class A, B, and C fires. How do they put out the fire?

9. What should a ramp technician keep in mind as aircraft taxi in his area of work?

10. Why should an aircraft be tied down after each flight?

Section B
Exercises

1. You are approaching a helicopter while the blades are turning, you should observe which precautions?

2. An aircraft comes in and parks, you need to secure it, explain how to do this task.

3. You have been asked to serve as a fire guard during the starting of a reciprocating engine, what will be your duties?

4. An aircraft has just been parked and the tow bar removed, what other action should take place next?

PAGE LEFT BLANK INTENTIONALLY

Section C
Final Chapter Exam - Multiple Choice

1. The color of 100LL fuel is _____
   - ☐ A. blue.
   - ☐ B. colorless or straw.
   - ☐ C. red.

2. What must accompany fuel vaporization?
   - ☐ A. Absorption of heat.
   - ☐ B. Decrease in vapor pressure.
   - ☐ C. Reduction in volume.

3. A fuel that vaporizes too readily may cause _____
   - ☐ A. hard starting.
   - ☐ B. detonation.
   - ☐ C. vapor lock.

4. The main differences between grades 100 and 100LL fuel are _____
   - ☐ A. volatility and lead content.
   - ☐ B. volatility, lead content, and color.
   - ☐ C. lead content and color.

5. Tetraethyl lead is added to aviation gasoline to _____
   - ☐ A. retard the formation of corrosives.
   - ☐ B. improve the gasoline's performance in the engine.
   - ☐ C. dissolve the moisture in the gasoline.

6. How are aviation fuels, which possess greater antiknock qualities than 100 octane, classified?
   - ☐ A. According to the milliliters of lead.
   - ☐ B. By reference to normal heptane.
   - ☐ C. By performance numbers.

7. What effect, if any, will aviation gasoline mixed with jet fuel have on a turbine engine?
   - ☐ A. No appreciable effect.
   - ☐ B. The tetraethyl lead in the gasoline forms deposits on the turbine blades.
   - ☐ C. The tetraethyl lead in the gasoline forms deposits on the compressor blades.

8. When towing a large aircraft _____
   - ☐ A. a person should be in the cockpit to watch for obstructions.
   - ☐ B. persons should be stationed at the nose, each wingtip, and the empennage at all times.
   - ☐ C. a person should be in the cockpit to operate the brakes.

9. When first starting to move an aircraft while taxiing, it is important to always _____
   - ☐ A. test the brakes.
   - ☐ B. closely monitor the instruments.
   - ☐ C. notify the control tower.

10. When taxiing an airplane with a quartering tailwind, the elevators and _____
    - ☐ A. upwind aileron should be held in the up position.
    - ☐ B. upwind aileron should be held in the down position.
    - ☐ C. both ailerons should be kept in the neutral position.

11. A person should approach or leave a helicopter in the pilot's field of vision whenever the engine is running in order to avoid _____
    - ☐ A. the tail rotor.
    - ☐ B. the main rotor.
    - ☐ C. blowing dust or debris caused by rotor downwash.

12. Which statement(s) is/are true regarding tie-down of small aircraft?
    01. Manila (hemp) rope has a tendency to stretch when it gets wet.
    02. Nylon or dacron rope is preferred to manila rope.
    03. Aircaft should be headed downwind in order to eliminate or minimize wing lift.
    04. Leave the nosewheel or tailwheel unlocked.
    ☐ A. 01, 02, 03, and 04
    ☐ B. 01 and 02
    ☐ C. 02

13. Which of the following is the most satisfactory extinguishing agent for use on a carburetor or intake fire?
    ☐ A. Dry chemical.
    ☐ B. A fine, water mist.
    ☐ C. Carbon dioxide.

14. If a radial engine has been shut down for more than 30 minutes, the propeller should be rotated through at least two revolutions to _____
    ☐ A. check for hydraulic lock.
    ☐ B. check for leaks.
    ☐ C. prime the engine.

15. The priming of a fuel injected horizontally opposed engine is accomplished by placing the fuel control lever in the _____
    ☐ A. IDLE CUTOFF position.
    ☐ B. AUTO RICH position.
    ☐ C. FULL RICH position.

16. How is a flooded engine, equipped with a float type carburetor, cleared of excessive fuel?
    ☐ A. Crank the engine with the starter or by hand, with the mixture control in cutoff, ignition switch off, and the throttle fully open, until the fuel charge has been cleared.
    ☐ B. Turn off the fuel and the ignition. Discontinue the starting attempt until the excess fuel has cleared.
    ☐ C. Crank the engine with the starter or by hand, with the mixture control in cutoff, ignition switch on, and the throttle fully open, until the excess fuel has cleared or until the engine starts.

17. Generally, when an induction fire occurs during starting of a reciprocating engine, the first course of action should be to _____
    ☐ A. discharge carbon dioxide from a fire extinguisher into the air intake of the engine.
    ☐ B. continue cranking and start the engine if possible.
    ☐ C. close the throttle.

18. Which of the following conditions has the most potential for causing engine damage when starting or attempting to start a turbine engine?
    ☐ A. Hung start.
    ☐ B. Cold start.
    ☐ C. Hot start.

Section A
Study Aid Questions - Multiple Choice

1. In what year did the Federal Aviation Agency become the Federal Aviation Administration?
   - ☐ A. 1988
   - ☐ B. 1966
   - ☐ C. 1934

2. SFAR is an acronym for?
   - ☐ A. Specific Federal Air Regulations.
   - ☐ B. Suspended Federal Air Regulations.
   - ☐ C. Special Federal Air Regulations.

3. FAR Part 43 relates to; Maintenance, preventative maintenance, rebuilding and alteration.
   - ☐ A. True
   - ☐ B. False
   - ☐ C. Cannot be determined.

4. 14 CFR Part 21 relates to what procedures?
   - ☐ A. Certification procedures for products and parts.
   - ☐ B. Continued airworthiness procedures for rotorcraft.
   - ☐ C. Obtaining airworthiness certificates.

5. 14 CFR Part 27 relates to what procedures?
   - ☐ A. Airworthiness Standards, light fixed wing aircraft.
   - ☐ B. Airworthiness Standards, engines and propellers.
   - ☐ C. Airworthiness Standards, normal category Rotorcraft.

6. Airworthiness directives address what issue?
   - ☐ A. Failure of aircraft components due to unusual circumstances.
   - ☐ B. Failure of aircraft components due to unanticipated problems in day to day use.
   - ☐ C. Failure of aircraft components with design life limited schedules and routine repairs.

7. Parts manufactured for installation on certified aircraft utilizing the PMA approval process must have the part number clearly and legibly marked on them?
   - ☐ A. True
   - ☐ B. False
   - ☐ C. Cannot be determined.

8. 14 CFR Part 65 contains information for certification of _____
   - ☐ A. airmen other than repair station employees.
   - ☐ B. airman other than designated mechanics.
   - ☐ C. airmen other than flight crew members.

9. An example of an airmen, other than a flight crewmember, would be _____
   - ☐ A. a mechanic.
   - ☐ B. a parachute jumper.
   - ☐ C. a first officer or copilot.

10. Compensation for direct and indirect expenses related to flight of an aircraft is referred to as _____
    - ☐ A. for sale.
    - ☐ B. a lease.
    - ☐ C. for hire.

11. Part 121 aircraft operations must have which of the following personnel on staff?
    - ☐ A. Director of maintenance.
    - ☐ B. Director of ground service.
    - ☐ C. Director of air traffic control.

12. Part 121.368 relates to _____
    - ☐ A. inspection of heavy aircraft.
    - ☐ B. inspection of aging aircraft.
    - ☐ C. inspection of rotorcraft.

13. Some regulations exclude aircraft operated in Alaska.
    - ☐ A. True
    - ☐ B. False
    - ☐ C. Cannot be determined.

14. A technical person examiner is an FAA employee and tests applicants for the mechanic certificate.
    - ☐ A. True
    - ☐ B. False
    - ☐ C. Cannot be determined.

15. Pilots may perform maintenance to rotorcraft in remote areas, within certain specific restrictions?
    - ☐ A. True
    - ☐ B. False
    - ☐ C. Cannot be determined.

16. Returning an aircraft to service after inspection or maintenance will _____
    - ☐ A. require a maintenance record entry.
    - ☐ B. always require a test flight.
    - ☐ C. never require a test flight.

17. If a major repair is performed without previously approved data, a _____ may be applied for from the FAA.
    - ☐ A. certificate
    - ☐ B. Supplemental Type Authority
    - ☐ C. Field Approval

18. A certificated private pilot can sign return to service documents?
    - ☐ A. True
    - ☐ B. False
    - ☐ C. Cannot be determined.

19. AC 43.13 is an Advisory Circular that pertains to acceptable techniques and practices for aircraft repairs and alterations.
    - ☐ A. True
    - ☐ B. False
    - ☐ C. Cannot be determined.

20. 14 CFR Part 91 covers operation of aircraft and flight rules. Therefore, it is of no use to maintenance technicians.
    - ☐ A. True
    - ☐ B. False
    - ☐ C. Cannot be determined.

Section B
Knowledge Application Questions
Short Answers

1. A person is working as a mechanic for a local airport. The person wants to know how to record a major alteration to the fuselage of an aircraft. This information will be found in which part of the regulations?

2. Which part of the regulations cover persons authorized to perform maintenance on certified aircraft in the United States?

3. A technician encounters damage to the underside of the wing of a light aircraft. The maintenance manuals for this aircraft do not contain any information regarding this type of repair. What reference may be used to complete the repair?

4. ATC Transponders are required to be tested periodically by which regulation?

5. The FAA form 337 is required to be completed in which situations?

6. Part 39, Airworthiness Directives, are issued in what circumstances?

7. The Type Certificate Data Sheet (TCDS) for an aircraft contains what type of information?

8. A Service Bulletin (SB) originates from what source?

9. What are the two categories of Light Sport Aircraft?

10. A technician performs a major alteration to the tail skin of a Light Sport Aircraft. This alteration will require evaluation relative to what?

Chapter 2, Section B - Regulations, Maintenance Forms, Records, and Publications

Name:_____   Date:_____

PAGE LEFT BLANK INTENTIONALLY

Section C
Final Chapter Exam - Multiple Choice

1. The fifth volume of the Code of Federal Regulations is devoted to _____
   - ☐ A. Light Sport Aircraft.
   - ☐ B. NASA.
   - ☐ C. NTSB.

2. A form 337 would be required when performing a major alteration to a Light Sport Aircraft?
   - ☐ A. True
   - ☐ B. False
   - ☐ C. Cannot be determined.

3. A radio station license is only required if the aircraft is operated outside of the borders of the United States.
   - ☐ A. True
   - ☐ B. False
   - ☐ C. Cannot be determined.

4. Supplemental Type Certificates primary deal with the _____ of certified aircraft.
   - ☐ A. flight
   - ☐ B. maintenance
   - ☐ C. modification

5. AC 43.13-1B excludes what type of aircraft?
   - ☐ A. Non-pressurized
   - ☐ B. Amphibious
   - ☐ C. Pressurized

6. 14 CFR Part 91 would be useful for a pilot, and maintenance technician, to reference for regulations concerning maintenance and operation of an aircraft.
   - ☐ A. True
   - ☐ B. False
   - ☐ C. Cannot be determined.

7. The aircraft weight that determines if it is classified as large, or small, is _____ pounds.
   - ☐ A. 11,000
   - ☐ B. 9,050
   - ☐ C. 12,500

8. Aircraft data plates must be permanently affixed to the aircraft and _____
   - ☐ A. Fireproof.
   - ☐ B. Painted.
   - ☐ C. Aluminum.

9. A large aircraft is damaged on the leading edge of the wing by a bird strike. The reference for the repair required would likely be found in the _____
   - ☐ A. Aircraft permanent records.
   - ☐ B. Aircraft operators manual.
   - ☐ C. Structural Repair Manual.

10. Suspected unapproved parts may include parts that are airworthy but lack proper paperwork to substantiate their airworthiness.
    - ☐ A. True
    - ☐ B. False
    - ☐ C. Cannot be determined.

Chapter 2, Section C - Regulations, Maintenance Forms, Records, and Publications

Name:_____ Date:_____

PAGE LEFT BLANK INTENTIONALLY

Section A
Study Aid Questions - Multiple Choice

1. Reviewing Chapter 1, list 3 possible applications of mathematics in aircraft maintenance.

    ☐ A. _____   ☐ B. _____   ☐ C. _____

2. Addition of whole numbers is best accomplished by arranging them _____
    ☐ A. from highest to lowest.
    ☐ B. in columns.
    ☐ C. from lowest to highest.

3. The result of multiplying whole numbers is called a _____
    ☐ A. product.
    ☐ B. sum.
    ☐ C. variant.

4. When dividing whole numbers, the results are called the _____ and the remainder.
    ☐ A. division
    ☐ B. factor
    ☐ C. quotient

5. When multiplying fractions, a common denominator may be found by multiplying all of the denominators together.
    ☐ A. True
    ☐ B. False
    ☐ C. Cannot be determined.

6. When dividing fractions, it is best to invert the second fraction and multiply the resulting numbers.
    ☐ A. True
    ☐ B. False
    ☐ C. Cannot be determined.

7. Reducing fractions is achieved when the numerator and denominator do not have any factors in common.
    ☐ A. True
    ☐ B. False
    ☐ C. Cannot be determined.

8. Which of the following is an example of a mixed number?
    ☐ A. 123
    ☐ B. .123
    ☐ C. 1 2/3

9. The decimal system has _____ digits.
    ☐ A. 12
    ☐ B. 16
    ☐ C. 10

10. When addition of decimal numbers is required, the decimals should be aligned vertically and according to place value.
    ☐ A. True
    ☐ B. False
    ☐ C. Cannot be determined.

11. When subtraction of decimal numbers is required, the decimals should be aligned vertically and according to place value.
    ☐ A. True
    ☐ B. False
    ☐ C. Cannot be determined.

12. When converting the fraction 21/64 to a decimal, the most correct result would be _____.
   ☐ A. .3281
   ☐ B. 3.047
   ☐ C. Cannot be determined.

13. 10:1 is an example of a ratio and may also be expressed as _____.
   ☐ A. 1/10, 10 to 1
   ☐ B. 1 to 10, 10/1
   ☐ C. 10/1, 10 to 1

14. The term percentage means?
   ☐ A. Parts per million.
   ☐ B. Parts out of one hundred.
   ☐ C. Parts per thousand.

15. 90% may also be expressed as one hundred parts out of ninety.
   ☐ A. True
   ☐ B. False
   ☐ C. Cannot be determined.

16. The sum of two negative numbers is a _____ number.
   ☐ A. negative
   ☐ B. positive
   ☐ C. zero

17. The product of two negative numbers is a _____ number.
   ☐ A. positive
   ☐ B. negative
   ☐ C. percentage

18. 4 to the power of 2 would equal _____.
   ☐ A. 2
   ☐ B. 8
   ☐ C. 16

19. Scientific notation is used to express very large or very small numbers.
   ☐ A. True
   ☐ B. False
   ☐ C. Cannot be determined.

20. Relationship of the length of the radius of a circle to its area is determined using a form of mathematics called _____
   ☐ A. quantum theory.
   ☐ B. algebra.
   ☐ C. decimal equivalents.

21. The area of a rectangle measuring 9 inches wide by 5 inches tall is _____ square inches.
   ☐ A. 54
   ☐ B. 45
   ☐ C. Cannot be determined.

22. The area of a triangle is determined by the formula: $A = \frac{1}{2} \times (base \times height)$.
   ☐ A. True
   ☐ B. False
   ☐ C. Cannot be determined.

23. An aircraft has a wingspan of 36 feet and a chord of 6 feet. What is the wing area?
   ☐ A. 6 square feet.
   ☐ B. 216 square feet.
   ☐ C. 216 linear feet.

24. The cubic volume of a solid rectangular object is determined with the formula?
    - ☐ A. length × width × height = volume of a solid object
    - ☐ B. radius squared × height = volume of a solid object
    - ☐ C. diameter + radius × height = square inches

25. The volume of a cylinder measuring 5 inches in diameter and 6 inches tall is _____
    - ☐ A. 47.1 cubic inches.
    - ☐ B. 94.2 cubic inches.
    - ☐ C. 117.75 cubic inches.

26. Trigonometric functions are used to show the relationship between the sides and angles of rectangles.
    - ☐ A. True
    - ☐ B. False
    - ☐ C. Cannot be determined.

27. Some examples of units used in the English measurement system include?
    - ☐ A. inch, foot, yard
    - ☐ B. inch, meter, rod
    - ☐ C. inch, kilometer, fraction

28. The binary number system is based on the fact that valves may be partially open or closed.
    - ☐ A. True
    - ☐ B. False
    - ☐ C. Cannot be determined.

29. The binary number system consists of the numbers -1, 0, and +1.
    - ☐ A. True
    - ☐ B. False
    - ☐ C. Cannot be determined.

30. The binary number system is most useful in aircraft electronics because those systems are _____.
    - ☐ A. ON/OFF
    - ☐ B. ON/OFF/ON
    - ☐ C. False/True/False

Chapter 3, Section A - Mathematics in Aviation Maintenance

Name:_____   Date:_____

PAGE LEFT BLANK INTENTIONALLY

Section B
Knowledge Application Questions
Short Answers

1. An aircraft baggage compartment has a maximum capacity of 100 pounds. The pilot loads the following items into the compartment. Has the maximum weight capacity been exceeded?
   01. Maps, logbooks, and calculator. (4 lbs)
   02. Tool bag with extra oil. (22 lbs)
   03. Personal travel items including clothes and toiletries. (32 lbs)
   04. Wheel chocks, tow bar, and engine inlet covers. (19 lbs)
   ☐ Yes   ☐ No

2. An unmanned aircraft has a range of 1,600 miles. What is the maximum distance from the point of takeoff that the aircraft can travel before the operator must begin the return trip to the point of takeoff?

3. An experimental aircraft fuel tank has a capacity of 40 gallons. If there are 4 quarts per gallon, how many quarts of gasoline may be placed into the fuel tank?

4. The maximum inflation pressure of an aircraft tire is 30 psi. If the tire is inflated to 2/3 capacity, what is the air pressure in the tire?

5. A pilot uses 6/8 of the length of a runway to takeoff. The runway is 2,700 feet long. How many feet of the runway remained at liftoff?

6. An aircraft painter completes 1/3 of a paint job on Monday, 1/4 of the job on Tuesday and finishes the job on Wednesday. How much of the job was finished on Wednesday?

7. An aircraft engine main bearing journal measures 3.258 inches outside diameter. The corresponding bearing inside diameter is 3.254 inches. What is the bearing clearance?

8. An aircraft engine cylinder has a volume at bottom dead center of 80 cubic inches. At top dead center the volume is 10 cubic inches. What is the compression ratio?

9. The cubic feet of warm air in a hot air balloon is 12 to the 4th power. How many cubic feet of air does this represent?

MATHEMATICS IN AVIATION MAINTENANCE

10. Using algebra and the following formula, determine the total capacitance of the aircraft electrical circuit where C1 = .2 microfarads, C2 = .9 microfarads, and C3 = .008 microfarads.

$$C_T = \frac{1}{\frac{1}{C_1} + \frac{1}{C_2} + \frac{1}{C_3}}$$

11. A grass runway in a rural community measures 3,000 feet long by 125 feet wide. For the purposes of paving the runway 6 inches deep, how many cubic yards of asphalt would be required?

12. A student pilot flies a triangular pattern on a long cross country trip. They fly straight East 100 miles, turn and fly straight North 45 miles, and then return to their home base. What is the total length of the trip?

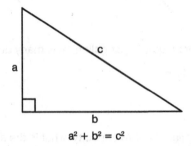

$$a^2 + b^2 = c^2$$

13. A 4 cylinder opposed aircraft engine has a bore of 6 inches and a stroke of 6 inches. What is the total cubic inch displacement of this engine?

14. A can of aircraft paint states on the label that the quantity is sufficient to cover 6 square feet of surface area. The object to be painted is a wheel pant which is approximately 32 inches long, 24 inches tall, and 10 inches wide. Will this quantity of paint be enough to complete the project?

15. The height of a tree at the end of a runway is required for a pilot to make a decision regarding aircraft takeoff distance and runway length needed. The pilot is standing 75 feet from the base of the tree and looking up at a 45 degree angle. How tall is the tree?

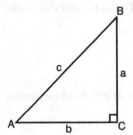

Section C
Final Chapter Exam - Multiple Choice

1. Ten aircraft at a flight school require 23 gallons of gasoline each. How many gallons is this?
   ☐ A. 2.3
   ☐ B. 230
   ☐ C. 2,300

2. The motor battery of an unmanned aircraft is 21% discharged. The capacity of the battery is 2,400 amps. How many amps remain in the battery?
   ☐ A. 1896 amps
   ☐ B. 189.6 amps
   ☐ C. 504 amps

3. A pilot flies .81 of the way to her destination. She then stops and refuels. How far does she have to go to complete her trip?
   ☐ A. Cannot be determined.
   ☐ B. 19 miles
   ☐ C. 19%

4. A piston engine has a volume of 10 cubic centimeters at bottom dead center of the piston travel and a volume of 1 cubic centimeter at top dead center of the piston travel. How would this be expressed?
   ☐ A. 10:1
   ☐ B. 1:10
   ☐ C. 10%

5. What is the square root of 49?
   ☐ A. 9
   ☐ B. 111001 binary
   ☐ C. 7

6. The operations inside parenthesis are always performed first in algebraic equations.
   ☐ A. True
   ☐ B. False
   ☐ C. Cannot be determined.

7. Length × Width × Height is the formula used to determine the volume of a solid rectangular radio bay.
   ☐ A. True
   ☐ B. False
   ☐ C. Cannot be determined.

8. The area of a triangular piece of sheet aluminum is determined by which of the following formulas?
   ☐ A. A = ½ (base × height × 90)
   ☐ B. A = ½ × (base × height)
   ☐ C. A = (base × height) + ½

9. Aircraft computers commonly use the binary numbering system for operation.
   ☐ A. True
   ☐ B. False
   ☐ C. Never

10. A sample binary number could include which of the following?
    ☐ A. 121102
    ☐ B. .001
    ☐ C. 1110011

Chapter 3, Section C - Mathematics in Aviation Maintenance

Name:_____   Date:_____

PAGE LEFT BLANK INTENTIONALLY

Section A
Study Aid Questions - Fill In The Blanks

1. Drawings made with the use of a computer are know as _____.

2. The process in which a computer is used in the design and drafting process is known as _____.

3. The process in which a computer is used in the engineering of a product is known as _____.

4. List the 4 basic types of drawings:

    _____   _____

    _____   _____

5. Every _____ must have some means of identification.

6. List 8 pieces of information contained in the title block of a drawing:

    _____   _____

    _____   _____

    _____   _____

    _____   _____

7. A _____ drawing shows an object as it appears to an observer.

8. _____ use a combination of the views of an orthographic projection and tilts the object forward so that portions of all three views can be seen in one view.

9. _____ diagrams are used mainly in troubleshooting.

10. _____ are used to illustrate a particular sequence or flow of events.

AIRCRAFT DRAWINGS

Section A
True or False

_____ 1. Drawings may be divided into three classes: detail, assembly, full section.

_____ 2. Drawing and prints are the link between the engineers who design an aircraft and the workers who build, maintain, and repair it.

_____ 3. Half sections are used to advantage with symmetrical objects to show only exterior views.

_____ 4. The universal numbering system provides a means of identifying standard drawing sizes.

_____ 5. Troubleshooting flowcharts are frequently used for the detection of faulty components.

Section A
Matching - Match the line types with their definition

_____ 1. A light solid line broken at the midpoint for insertion of measurement indications and having opposite pointing arrowheads at each end.

_____ 2. These lines are made up of alternate long and short dashes.

_____ 3. These lines are used to extend the line showing the side or edge of a figure for the purpose of placing a dimension to that side or edge.

_____ 4. This type of line is composed of one long and two short evenly spaced dashes.

_____ 5. These lines indicate the exposed surfaces of an object in a sectional view.

_____ 6. This line indicates that a portion of the object is not shown on the drawing.

_____ 7. These types of lines are used for all lines on the drawing representing visible lines on the object.

_____ 8. This type of line indicates invisible edges or contours.

_____ 9. This line uses a solid line with one arrowhead and indicates a part or portion to which a note, number, or other reference applies.

_____ 10. This line indicates stitching or sewing lines and consists of a series of evenly spaced dashes.

A. Center Line	E. Extension Line	I. Leader Line
B. Dimension Line	F. Break Line	J. Stitch Line
C. Phantom Line	G. Outline or Visible Line	
D. Sectioning Line	H. Hidden Line	

Name:_____   Date:_____

Section B
Short Answers

1. Describe the information that a drawing conveys to the person reading the drawing.

2. Explain tolerances as they pertain to drawings.

3. What does the term scale refer to on a drawing?

4. When using a digital image for transmitting information to others, what type of information should be included to help define the damaged area.

Section B
Exercises

1. (Using Figure 4-20 on page 4-17 of the textbook "Block Diagram") If the voltage selector was completely inoperative, would the power amplifier receive any signal?

2. (Using Figure 4-19 on page 4-16 of the textbook "Air Conditioning System for B-737NG") What are the two sources of cooling air when in flight?

3. (Using Figure 4-18 on page 4-15 of the textbook "Example of Installation Drawing") What component secures the altitude/vertical speed selector?

4. (Using Figure 4-33 on page 4-27 of the textbook "Electrical Wiring Chart") In a 28 volt system with a required 50 feet of bundled wire and a 15 amp load, determine the required wire size.

AIRCRAFT DRAWINGS

5. (Using Figure 4-32 on page 4-26 of the textbook "Nomogram") What is the specific weight of Jet A at 10°C in pounds per gallon?

6. Use the Figure below to identify the lines used in the drawing.

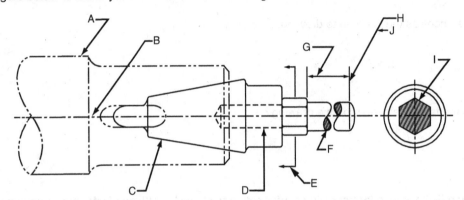

A. _____   F. _____

B. _____   G. _____

C. _____   H. _____

D. _____   I. _____

E. _____   J. _____

Name:_____   Date:_____

8083-30B-ATB General Workbook

Section C
Final Chapter Exam - Multiple Choice

1. Regarding the following statements: (1) Schematic diagrams indicate the location of individual components in the aircraft. (2) Schematic diagrams indicate the location of components with respect to each other within the system.
   - ☐ A. Only No. 1 is true.
   - ☐ B. Both No. 1 and No. 2 are true.
   - ☐ C. Only No. 2 is true.

2. For sketching purposes, almost all objects are composed of one or some combination of six basic shapes. These include?
   - ☐ A. Angle, arc, line, plane, square, and circle.
   - ☐ B. Triangle, circle, cube, cylinder, cone, and sphere.
   - ☐ C. Triangle, plane, circle, line, square, and sphere.

3. Regarding the following statements: (1) According to 14 CFR Part 91, repairs to an aircraft's skin should have a detailed dimensional sketch included in the permanent records. (2) On occasion, a mechanic may need to make a simple sketch of a proposed repair to an aircraft, a new design, or a modification.
   - ☐ A. Only No. 1 is true.
   - ☐ B. Only No. 2 is true.
   - ☐ C. Both No. 1 and No. 2 are true.

4. What are the proper procedural steps for sketching repairs and alterations?
   - ☐ A. Add dimensions, add detail, block in, darken views.
   - ☐ B. Add detail, darken views, block in, add dimensions.
   - ☐ C. Block in, add detail, darken view, add dimensions.

5. What should be the first step of the procedure in sketching an aircraft wing skin repair?
   - ☐ A. Draw heavy guidelines.
   - ☐ B. Lay out the repair.
   - ☐ C. Block in the views.

6. What is the class of working drawing that is the description/depiction of a single part?
   - ☐ A. Installation drawing.
   - ☐ B. Assembly drawing.
   - ☐ C. Detail drawing.

7. In the reading of aircraft blueprints, the term 'tolerance', used in association with aircraft parts or components;
   - ☐ A. is the tightest permissible fit for proper construction and operation of mating parts.
   - ☐ B. is the difference between extreme permissible dimensions that a part may have and still be acceptable.
   - ☐ C. represents the limit of galvanic compatibility between different adjoining material types in aircraft parts.

8. Regarding the following statements: (1) A measurement should not be scaled from an aircraft print because the paper shrinks or stretches when the print is made. (2) When a detail drawing is made, it is carefully and accurately drawn to scale, and is dimensioned.
   - ☐ A. Only No. 2 is true.
   - ☐ B. Both No. 1 and No. 2 are true.
   - ☐ C. Neither No. 1 nor No. 2 is true.

9. A drawing in which the sub-assemblies or parts are shown as brought together on the aircraft is called _____
   - ☐ A. an assembly drawing.
   - ☐ B. an installation drawing.
   - ☐ C. a detail drawing.

10. In what type of electrical diagrams are images of components used instead of conventional electrical symbols?
    - ☐ A. Pictorial diagram.
    - ☐ B. Schematic diagram.
    - ☐ C. Block diagram.

AIRCRAFT DRAWINGS

11. Which statement is true regarding an orthographic projection?
    ☐ A. There are always at least two views.
    ☐ B. It could have as many as eight views.
    ☐ C. One view, two view, and three view drawings are the most common.

12. Which of the following terms is/are used to indicate specific measured distances from the datum and/or other points identified by the manufacturer, to points in or on the aircraft?
    01. Zone Numbers
    02. Reference Numbers
    03. Station Numbers
    ☐ A. 01 and 03
    ☐ B. 02
    ☐ C. 03

Section A
Study Aid Questions - Fill In The Blanks

1. Physics is sometimes called the science of _____ and _____ .

2. _____ is the foundation of any discussion of physics.

3. _____ is the force acting mutually between particles of matter.

4. A device called a _____ is used for measuring specific gravity of _____ .

5. Stored energy or energy at rest is defined as _____ .

6. Energy that is in motion is defined as _____ .

7. If a _____ is applied, the tendency will be for the object to move.

8. Two factors are involved with measurable work, they are _____ and _____ .

9. The force of friction for objects mounted on wheels or rollers is called _____ .

10. The concept of power involves work but adds the consideration of _____ .

PHYSICS FOR AVIATION

Section A
True or False

_____ 1. Torque is described as a force acting along a distance.

_____ 2. To calculate torque it is power × distance.

_____ 3. A machine is any device with which work may be accomplished.

_____ 4. Pulleys are simple machines that are used as second class levers.

_____ 5. A single fixed pulley has the mechanical advantage of 2.

_____ 6. A single moveable pulley has the mechanical advantage of 2.

_____ 7. The gear with the input force is called the drive gear.

_____ 8. Stress is typically measured in pounds per square foot or pounds per square inch.

_____ 9. Compression is the stress an object experiences when it is twisted.

_____ 10. Tension is a force that tries to pull an object apart.

_____ 11. When an object becomes distorted by an applied force, the object is said to be strained.

_____ 12. Heat is a form of energy.

_____ 13. Chemical energy includes all methods of producing increase motion of molecules such as friction, impact of bodies, or compression of gases.

_____ 14. The two ways that are used to express quantities of heat energy are the calorie and the BTU (British Thermal Unit).

_____ 15. An aircraft air-cooled piston engine is a good example of convection being used to transfer heat.

_____ 16. Thermal expansion is the amount of force acting on a specific amount of surface area.

_____ 17. A gauge that includes atmospheric pressure in its reading is measuring what is known as absolute pressure or PSIA.

_____ 18. The pivot point is called the fulcrum of a lever.

_____ 19. A deflecting beam torque wrench measures strain by using a pressure gauge.

_____ 20. The three methods of heat transfer are conduction, convection, and radiation.

Section A
Matching

1. Pure water boils: Celsius _____ , Kelvin _____ , Fahrenheit _____ , Rankine _____ .
2. Pure water freezes: Celsius _____ , Kelvin _____ , Fahrenheit _____ , Rankine _____ .
3. Molecular motion ceases at absolute zero: Celsius _____ , Fahrenheit _____ .

A. 100	C. -273	E. 373	G. 492	I. 273
B. 0	D. 212	F. 672	H. 32	J. -460

Chapter 5, Section A - Physics for Aviation

Name:_____ Date:_____

Section B
Knowledge Application Questions - Matching

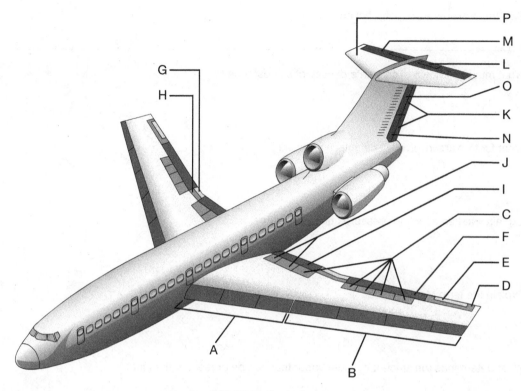

Boeing 727 Flight Controls

Identify the following Flight Controls using the Figure above.

A. _____   E. _____   I. _____   M. _____

B. _____   F. _____   J. _____   N. _____

C. _____   G. _____   K. _____   O. _____

D. _____   H. _____   L. _____   P. _____

Identify the following Wing Terminology using the Figure below.

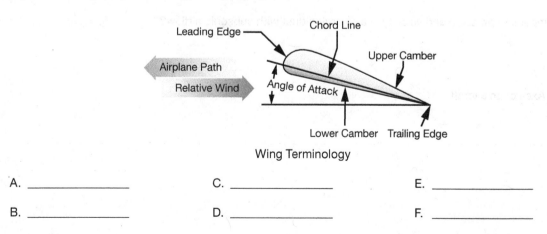

Wing Terminology

A. _____   C. _____   E. _____

B. _____   D. _____   F. _____

PHYSICS FOR AVIATION

Section B
Short Answers

1. Give three examples of potential energy.

   1. _____ 2. _____ 3. _____

2. What must be known to calculate density of a substance?

3. What factors are involved in calculating power?

4. Explain what an absolute pressure gauge measures.

5. Explain the term Mach number.

6. What determines the amount of water vapor that can be present in the air?

7. List the four forces of flight.

   1. _____ 3. _____

   2. _____ 4. _____

8. What happens to pressure and velocity in a converging duct with subsonic airflow?

9. What happens to pressure and velocity in a diverging duct with subsonic airflow?

10. List the Axes of an aircraft.

    1. _____ 2. _____ 3. _____

11. How is control obtained about the longitudinal axis?

12. Describe relative wind as it pertains to an aircraft in flight.

13. What forces must be equal for a helicopter to hover?

14. What is the flight condition of a helicopter known as autorotation?

15. Discuss the solution to blade dissymmetry of lift.

Section B
Exercises

1. Calculate the work done if 300 lbs. is moved 50 feet.

2. If a force of 550 lbs. is applied at a distance of 150 ft. in 3 min., how much power is being produced?

3. Convert 27,500 ft. lbs. per minute to horsepower.

4. If a piston has a force of 400 lbs. on it and the connecting rod attaches at an offset of 5 inches, what is the amount of torque being supplied?

5. An effort is being placed on a first class lever of X lbs. at 24 inches from the fulcrum. On the other side of the fulcrum is a resistance of 600 lbs. at a distance of 12 inches. What would be the mechanical advantage?

Chapter 5, Section B - Physics for Aviation

Name:_____   Date:_____

PAGE LEFT BLANK INTENTIONALLY

Section C
Final Chapter Exam - Multiple Choice

1. What is the piston displacement of a master cylinder with a 1.5-inch diameter bore and a piston stroke of 4 inches?
   - ☐ A. 9.4247 cubic inches.
   - ☐ B. 7.0686 cubic inches.
   - ☐ C. 6.1541 cubic inches.

2. A four cylinder aircraft engine has a cylinder bore of 3.78-inches and is 8.5-inches deep. With the piston on bottom center, the top of the piston measures 4-inches from the bottom of the cylinder. What is the approximate piston displacement of this engine?
   - ☐ A. 200 cubic inches.
   - ☐ B. 360 cubic inches.
   - ☐ C. 235 cubic inches.

3. What force is exerted on the piston in a hydraulic cylinder if the area of the piston is 1.2 square inches and the fluid pressure is 850 psi?
   - ☐ A. 1,020 pounds
   - ☐ B. 960 pounds
   - ☐ C. 850 pounds

4. What size sheet of metal is required to fabricate a cylinder 20" long by 8" in diameter? (Note: C = pi × D)
   - ☐ A. 20 inches × 25-5/32 inches
   - ☐ B. 20 inches × 24-9/64 inches
   - ☐ C. 20 inches × 25-9/64 inches

5. If the temperature of a confined liquid is held constant and its pressure is tripled, the volume will be _____
   - ☐ A. triple.
   - ☐ B. be reduced to one third its original volume.
   - ☐ C. remain the same.

6. The speed of sound in the atmosphere is most affected by variations in which of the following _____
   - ☐ A. sound frequency (cycles per second).
   - ☐ B. ambient temperature.
   - ☐ C. barometric pressure.

7. Which will weigh the least?
   - ☐ A. 98 parts of dry air and 2 parts of water vapor.
   - ☐ B. 35 parts of dry air and 65 parts of water vapor.
   - ☐ C. 50 parts of dry air and 50 parts of water vapor.

8. Under which conditions will the rate of flow of a liquid through a metering orifice (or jet) be the greatest (all other factors being equal)?
   - ☐ A. Unmetered pressure, 18 psi; Metered pressure, 17.5 psi; Atmospheric pressure, 14.5 psi
   - ☐ B. Unmetered pressure, 23 psi; Metered pressure, 12 psi; Atmospheric pressure, 14.3 psi
   - ☐ C. Unmetered pressure, 17 psi; Metered pressure, 5 psi; Atmospheric pressure, 14.7 psi

9. The boiling point of a given liquid varies _____
   - ☐ A. directly with pressure.
   - ☐ B. inversely with pressure.
   - ☐ C. directly with density.

10. How much work input is required to lower (not drop) a 120-pound weight from the top of a 3-foot table to the floor?
    - ☐ A. 120 pounds of force
    - ☐ B. 360 foot-pounds
    - ☐ C. 40 foot-pounds

PHYSICS FOR AVIATION

11. An airplane wing is designed to produce lift resulting from _____
    - ☐ A. positive air pressure below and above the wing surface along with downward deflection of air.
    - ☐ B. negative air pressure below the wing's surface and positive air pressure above the wing's surface along with the downward deflection of air.
    - ☐ C. positive air pressure below the wing's surface and negative air pressure above the wing's surface along with the downward deflection of air.

12. A wing with a very high aspect ratio (in comparison with a low aspect ratio wing) will have _____
    - ☐ A. increased drag at high angles of attack.
    - ☐ B. a low stall speed.
    - ☐ C. poor control qualities at low airspeeds.

13. The purpose of aircraft wing dihedral is to _____
    - ☐ A. increase lateral stability.
    - ☐ B. increase longitudinal stability.
    - ☐ C. increase lift coefficient of the wing.

14. If all, or a significant part of a stall strip is missing on an airplane wing, a likely result will be _____
    - ☐ A. decreased lift in the area of installation at high angles of attack.
    - ☐ B. asymmetrical lateral control at low angles of attack.
    - ☐ C. asymmetrical lateral control at or near stall angles of attack.

15. Which statement concerning heat and/or temperature is true?
    - ☐ A. There is an inverse relationship between temperature and heat.
    - ☐ B. Temperature is a measure of the kinetic energy of the molecules of any substance.
    - ☐ C. Temperature is a measure of the potential energy of the molecules of any substance.

16. In physics, which of the following factors are necessary to determine power?
    - 01. Force Exerted
    - 02. Distance Moved
    - 03. Time Required
    - ☐ A. 01 and 02
    - ☐ B. 02 and 03
    - ☐ C. 01, 02, and 03

17. Aspect ratio of a wing is defined as the ratio of _____
    - ☐ A. wingspan to the wing root.
    - ☐ B. square of the chord to the wingspan.
    - ☐ C. wingspan to the mean chord.

AIRCRAFT WEIGHT AND BALANCE

6

Section A
Study Aid Questions - Fill In The Blanks, Multiple Choice, True or False

1. The weight of an aircraft, and how that weight is distributed, or balanced, is important for _____ and _____ .

2. A heavy aircraft with a small wing will require relatively _____ airspeeds for takeoff.
   - ☐ A. High
   - ☐ B. Low
   - ☐ C. Cannot be determined.

3. Aircraft weight must be considered, as well as the balance point of that weight. An aircraft that is nose heavy will require excessive control deflections, and increased control pressures, to control the aircraft. This results in increased drag and fuel burn.
   - ☐ A. True
   - ☐ B. False
   - ☐ C. Cannot be determined.

4. An aircraft balanced so that the center of gravity, and the center of _____, are close to each other is in optimum balance.
   - ☐ A. the fuselage
   - ☐ B. the tail
   - ☐ C. lift

5. Each aircraft that is manufactured receives a weight and balance report to become part of the?
   - ☐ A. Aircraft data plate.
   - ☐ B. Aircraft bill of sale.
   - ☐ C. Aircraft records.

6. Adding equipment such as radios, or GPS receivers, will require the weight and balance records be _____
   - ☐ A. revised to reflect the change.
   - ☐ B. sent to the faa.
   - ☐ C. discarded.

7. The datum of an aircraft is _____
   - ☐ A. determined by the owner and may be changed periodically.
   - ☐ B. an imaginary vertical plane for reference during weight and balance calculations.
   - ☐ C. an acronym for performance increases from various weight changes.

8. The term arm, in relation to weight and balance, is _____
   - ☐ A. A horizontal distance from the datum in inches + or –.
   - ☐ B. A vertical distance from the datum to a particular piece of equipment.
   - ☐ C. A horizontal distance from the spinner to the front seat.

9. The term moment, in relation to aircraft weight and balance, is _____
   - ☐ A. the sum of the arm and datum.
   - ☐ B. the sum of the weight and the arm.
   - ☐ C. the product of the weight and arm.

10. The center of gravity is _____
    - ☐ A. a point on the aircraft, if lifted at that point, an aircraft would hang level.
    - ☐ B. the point on the aircraft that represents the sum of the arms.
    - ☐ C. the point ahead of the aircraft that measurements are taken from.

11. Maximum, or gross weight, varies from empty weight in that _____
    - ☐ A. Maximum weight includes empty weight and useful load items.
    - ☐ B. Maximum weight cannot be determined.
    - ☐ C. Useful load cannot be determined.

8083-30B-ATB General Workbook

37

AIRCRAFT WEIGHT AND BALANCE

12. Fuel and baggage are considered part of the _____
    - ☐ A. useful load.
    - ☐ B. empty weight center of gravity.
    - ☐ C. Cannot be determined.

13. Tare weight is subtracted from the weight shown on the scales and usually consists of chocks, jacks or other equipment used to level, or secure, the aircraft.
    - ☐ A. True
    - ☐ B. False
    - ☐ C. Cannot be determined.

14. The most important reason for performing a weight and balance procedure on an aircraft is _____
    - ☐ A. determining tare weight.
    - ☐ B. determining gross weight.
    - ☐ C. determining empty weight and empty weight center of gravity.

15. Calculating the _____ for each scale reading is the most practical way to determine aircraft weight and balance.
    - ☐ A. arm length
    - ☐ B. moment sum
    - ☐ C. moment value

16. To determine center of gravity the following formula is used:
    - ☐ A. total arm × total weight.
    - ☐ B. total moment ÷ total weight.
    - ☐ C. total moment × total weight.

17. Center of gravity is defined as the point that all _____ are equal.
    - ☐ A. arms
    - ☐ B. moments
    - ☐ C. datums

18. One location for weight and balance information, for a particular aircraft, is the Type Certificate Data Sheets.
    - ☐ A. True
    - ☐ B. False
    - ☐ C. Cannot be determined.

19. Aircraft maximum, or gross weight, must be known to safely operate an aircraft and can usually be found in the Type Certificate Data Sheets.
    - ☐ A. True
    - ☐ B. False
    - ☐ C. Cannot be determined.

20. Two types of scales are used to weigh aircraft. What are they?
    - ☐ A. Motorized and linear.
    - ☐ B. Mechanical and electronic.
    - ☐ C. Scales are not commonly used in aviation.

21. Load cell scales are commonly found to be the platform type and placed on top of the aircraft _____
    - ☐ A. fuselage.
    - ☐ B. wing.
    - ☐ C. jacks.

22. The aircraft must be _____ in order to perform weighing operations.
    - ☐ A. level
    - ☐ B. fully loaded
    - ☐ C. outside

23. Unusable fuel is included in the aircraft empty weight.
    - ☐ A. True
    - ☐ B. False
    - ☐ C. Cannot be determined.

24. _____ weigh an aircraft with partially filled fuel tanks.
    - ☐ A. Never
    - ☐ B. Always
    - ☐ C. Sometimes

25. Typical aircraft weighing points are _____
    - ☐ A. wings, tail, and fuselage.
    - ☐ B. jack locations, or tires in the case of platform type scales.
    - ☐ C. fuselage only.

26. A center of gravity range is the forward and aft limits within which the aircraft must balance.
    - ☐ A. True
    - ☐ B. False
    - ☐ C. Cannot be determined.

27. An equipment change from an older, heavier radio to a newer light weight system will require _____
    - ☐ A. the aircraft be test flown to determine adverse handling conditions.
    - ☐ B. the pilot to be notified in writing within 30 days.
    - ☐ C. the aircraft weight and balance records be updated accordingly.

28. Ballast may be used in an aircraft to obtain the desired balance condition for safe operation. Ballast may be temporary or permanent in nature.
    - ☐ A. True
    - ☐ B. False
    - ☐ C. Cannot be determined.

29. Helicopters have _____ and _____ center of gravity limits.
    - ☐ A. fore and aft
    - ☐ B. vertical and horizontal
    - ☐ C. longitudinal and lateral

30. _____ is used when establishing center of gravity for aircraft with tapered and/or swept back wings.
    - ☐ A. Mean aerodynamic chord
    - ☐ B. Mean average span
    - ☐ C. Percent constant chord

Chapter 6, Section A - Aircraft Weight and Balance

Name:_____   Date:_____

PAGE LEFT BLANK INTENTIONALLY

Section B
Knowledge Application Questions
Short Answers

1. A tailwheel type aircraft is placed on scales for weighing and leveled. The weight of the tail stand is 25 pounds and it is placed on top of the rear scale. The rear scale reads 235 pounds. What is the actual tail weight used in the weight and balance calculations?

2. A pilot fuels and loads an aircraft for a cross country trip. He finds when doing the weight and balance calculations that the aircraft is out of the safe Center Of Gravity (CG) range forward. The pilot moves some baggage towards the tail of the aircraft. Will this help or hinder the proper CG location?

3. A UAS with tricycle landing gear is weighed and the following results obtained: Nose wheel 274 pounds, left main gear 435 pounds, and right main gear 434 pounds. The datum is ahead of the aircraft 14 inches. It is 34 inches from the datum to the nose wheel and 67 inches from the nose wheel to the main gear. What is the empty weight center of gravity?

4. The UAS in question 3 is then fueled for flight with 50 gallons of gasoline. The fuel tank is 55 inches aft of the datum. What is the new center of gravity for the UAS?

5. A light aircraft weighs 2,767 pounds empty weight and the center of gravity is 34 inches aft of the leading edge of the wing. The datum is the firewall which is 48 inches ahead of the leading edge. A new engine is installed that weighs 23 pounds less than the old engine. The engine weight is centered 22 inches ahead of the firewall. What is the new empty weight CG relative to the leading edge of the wing?

6. The empty weight CG of a helicopter is found to be out of limits to the rear of the aircraft according to the Type Certificate. What must be done prior to flight of this helicopter?

7. What two things must be known about a piece of equipment that is removed or added from an aircraft in order to perform weight and balance calculations?

8. An autonomous crop spraying aircraft has a tank capacity of 200 gallons of water. The tank is located on the center of gravity of the aircraft. The aircraft gross weight is 4,356 pounds. All the spray is applied to the field. What effect does this have on CG and how much does the aircraft now weigh?

AIRCRAFT WEIGHT AND BALANCE

9. An aircraft technician removes 2 radios from a light aircraft. The radios weigh 7 pounds each. The datum of the aircraft is the leading edge of the wing. The empty weight CG of the aircraft is 26.76 inches aft of the datum. The total empty weight of the aircraft is 2,556 pounds. What is the new empty weight CG for this aircraft?

10. Utilizing the graph below, a loaded aircraft weighs 2,230 pounds and has a moment of 92,000 in-lbs. Is this aircraft safe for flight in the Normal Category?

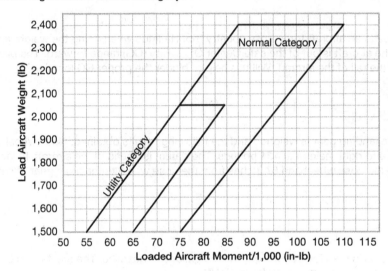

Section C
Final Chapter Exam - Multiple Choice, True or False

1. Weight and balance calculations are required to be performed on every aircraft and the results _____
   - ☐ A. provided to the pilot within 30 days.
   - ☐ B. noted in the repair station records.
   - ☐ C. recorded in the aircraft permanent records.

2. When weighing an aircraft, all items of _____ must be removed and the aircraft must be level.
   - ☐ A. useful load
   - ☐ B. tare
   - ☐ C. gross weight

3. The datum, for weight and balance purposes, is a vertical plane from which all horizontal measurements are taken for use in determining the arm of each item of weight.
   - ☐ A. True
   - ☐ B. False
   - ☐ C. Cannot be determined.

4. The arm of each item of weight is the vertical distance of that weight from the datum.
   - ☐ A. True
   - ☐ B. False
   - ☐ C. Cannot be determined.

5. A radio removed from ahead of the datum would have a positive moment.
   - ☐ A. True
   - ☐ B. False
   - ☐ C. Cannot be determined.

6. Aircraft weight and balance theory is based on the principles of _____
   - ☐ A. fulcrum.
   - ☐ B. pivot.
   - ☐ C. first class lever.

7. Usable fuel is considered part of the aircraft _____ for weight and balance purposes.
   - ☐ A. datum
   - ☐ B. useful load
   - ☐ C. empty weight

8. Weight × Arm = _____ in calculating aircraft weight and balance.
   - ☐ A. useful load
   - ☐ B. ballast
   - ☐ C. moment

9. The _____ is useful to determine equipment location and other information for weight and balance purposes.
   - ☐ A. Pilots Handbook
   - ☐ B. FAA Advisory Circular
   - ☐ C. Type Certificate Data Sheet

10. The standard weight of a person, for the purposes of weight and balance calculations, is _____
    - ☐ A. 180 pounds.
    - ☐ B. 170 pounds.
    - ☐ C. 180 kilos.

Chapter 6, Final Chapter Exam - Aircraft Weight and Balance

Name:_____ Date:_____

PAGE LEFT BLANK INTENTIONALLY

AIRCRAFT MATERIALS, HARDWARE, AND PROCESSES

Section A
Study Aid Questions - Multiple Choice, True or False

1. Aircraft metals must be _____ so that they can be formed and shaped without detrimental effect.
   - ☐ A. malleable
   - ☐ B. elastic
   - ☐ C. dense

2. Chrome-molybdenum steel, commonly used in aircraft construction, is an alloy of _____
   - ☐ A. carbon, tin, antimony.
   - ☐ B. carbon, molybdenum, tin.
   - ☐ C. carbon, molybdenum, chromium.

3. Aluminum is used widely in aircraft construction because it _____
   - ☐ A. is difficult to form but retains ductility.
   - ☐ B. is light, strong, and easily formed.
   - ☐ C. inexpensive and commonly available.

4. The metal Titanium, when moistened and drawn across glass, will produce a pencil like line.
   - ☐ A. True
   - ☐ B. False
   - ☐ C. Cannot be determined.

5. Normalizing is a term used to describe _____
   - ☐ A. relief of stress in an iron based alloy through the use of heat.
   - ☐ B. tempering process of using heat to soften metals.
   - ☐ C. relief of stress in copper based alloys through the use of extreme cold.

6. Heat treating is the process of using heating and cooling methods to obtain specific, and desirable, characteristics in metals.
   - ☐ A. True
   - ☐ B. False
   - ☐ C. Cannot be determined.

7. Typical terms used to describe heat treating methods include _____
   - ☐ A. heating, cooling, drawing, forming.
   - ☐ B. heating, cooling, soaking, quenching.
   - ☐ C. ductility, malleability, elastic limits.

8. Case hardening may be in the form of _____
   - ☐ A. carburizing, cyaniding, or nitriding.
   - ☐ B. nitrating, cycling, or quenching.
   - ☐ C. carburizing, neutralizing, or sanitizing.

9. Alclad aluminum is primarily _____
   - ☐ A. aluminum that has copper as an alloying agent.
   - ☐ B. aluminum that has undergone heat treatment.
   - ☐ C. aluminum that has pure aluminum on each side of an alloy core.

10. An 1100 aluminum alloy rivet is a soft rivet not suitable for high strength applications.
    - ☐ A. True
    - ☐ B. False
    - ☐ C. Cannot be determined.

11. The Rockwell Hardness Tester measures resistance to penetration of metals and is useful for determining _____
    ☐ A. heat treatment condition.
    ☐ B. pre-heat treatment condition.
    ☐ C. both A and B.

12. Casting, forging, and extruding are methods of heat treatment and determine the final hardness characteristics of metals.
    ☐ A. True
    ☐ B. False
    ☐ C. Cannot be determined.

13. Composite aircraft construction material is commonly _____
    ☐ A. a fiber material with a supporting resin.
    ☐ B. not used on aircraft.
    ☐ C. plastic.

14. Composite aircraft construction may involve toxic or hazardous materials as compared to metals.
    ☐ A. True
    ☐ B. False
    ☐ C. Cannot be determined.

15. Common aircraft structural fibers include _____
    ☐ A. aramid, fiberglass, and wood
    ☐ B. aramid, fiberglass, and graphite.
    ☐ C. aramid, fiberglass, and plastic.

16. The minimum safety equipment when grinding or cutting composite materials, to protect the technician's lungs, would include _____
    ☐ A. latex gloves, head covering, and steel toes shoes.
    ☐ B. latex gloves, and long sleeve shirt.
    ☐ C. a respirator with particle protection.

17. Barrier creams to protect the skin are acceptable for use when working with composites.
    ☐ A. True
    ☐ B. False
    ☐ C. Cannot be determined.

18. Honeycomb composite construction for aircraft would include _____
    ☐ A. a core, face sheets, and adhesive.
    ☐ B. a core, bees wax, and resin.
    ☐ C. a face sheet, resin, and fiberglass.

19. The term rubber may include _____
    ☐ A. natural rubber, synthetic rubber, and nitrate rubber.
    ☐ B. natural rubber, and synthetic rubber such as buna-s.
    ☐ C. all naturally occurring flexible substances.

20. A class three bolt thread is _____
    ☐ A. a tight fit.
    ☐ B. a loose fit.
    ☐ C. a medium fit.

21. An AN73 bolt has the head drilled for insertion of safety wire.
    ☐ A. True
    ☐ B. False
    ☐ C. Cannot be determined.

22. Aircraft bolts have identification information on the _____ of the bolt?
    ☐ A. shank
    ☐ B. shaft
    ☐ C. head

23. Aircraft nuts are made of _____
    ☐ A. copper plated carbon steel.
    ☐ B. copper plated nickel steel.
    ☐ C. cadmium plated carbon steel.

24. Self-locking nuts may be used on aircraft if _____
    ☐ A. the bolt or nut are not subject to rotation.
    ☐ B. not approved by the manufacturer.
    ☐ C. they are safety wired.

25. Sheet spring nuts are used in structural applications if approved by the manufacturer.
    ☐ A. True
    ☐ B. False
    ☐ C. Cannot be determined.

26. A helicoil insert is used _____
    ☐ A. to replace damaged rivets in aircraft structures.
    ☐ B. to replace damaged threads in aircraft structures.
    ☐ C. when the next smaller size bolt is desired.

27. Self plugging, friction lock, rivets are typically used when access to both sides of an aircraft surface is difficult or impossible.
    ☐ A. True
    ☐ B. False
    ☐ C. Cannot be determined.

28. The three parts of a Camloc aircraft fastener include _____
    ☐ A. stud, grommet, head.
    ☐ B. stud, head, receptacle.
    ☐ C. stud, grommet, receptacle.

29. One of the most common aircraft cables is a 7 × 19. What do these numbers mean?
    ☐ A. The tensile strength is the product of 7 and 19.
    ☐ B. The cable may be used in a 7 × 19 area.
    ☐ C. The cable is made up of 7 strands of wire with 19 wires in each.

30. Safety wire is commonly used on aircraft to secure fasteners. It must be installed _____
    ☐ A. so that movement of the fastener tends to tighten the wire.
    ☐ B. so that movement of the fastener tends to loosen the wire.
    ☐ C. so that movement of the wire tends to loosen the fastener.

Chapter 7, Section A - Aircraft Materials, Hardware, and Processes

Name:_____ Date:_____

PAGE LEFT BLANK INTENTIONALLY

AIRCRAFT MATERIALS, HARDWARE, AND PROCESSES

Section B
Knowledge Application Questions
Short Answers

1. The series designation 45XX is used for which alloyed steel?

2. 1100 aluminum contains which specific alloy materials?

3. What natural characteristic of metals is dangerous to aircraft due to the thin material thicknesses involved?

4. The color orange indicates a metal temperature approximately how many degrees Fahrenheit?

5. The normalizing temperature for common 4130 aircraft steel is _____ degrees F.

6. Hardening of 51335 steel is accomplished at _____ degrees F.

7. Alloy 6061 T4 aluminum is quenched in what medium for solution heat treatment purposes?

8. A triangle placed on the head of an aircraft bolt indicates what specific characteristic.

9. A "wing" nut is designated with which AN number?

10. A 5056T rivet would be indicated by what head markings?

Chapter 7, Section B - Aircraft Materials, Hardware, and Processes

Name:_____ Date:_____

PAGE LEFT BLANK INTENTIONALLY

AIRCRAFT MATERIALS, HARDWARE, AND PROCESSES

1. An aircraft landing gear would require what metallic property in order to avoid deformation?
    - ☐ A. Permeability
    - ☐ B. Density
    - ☐ C. Strength

2. An aircraft bracket, having iron as its primary element, would be described as nonferrous.
    - ☐ A. True
    - ☐ B. False
    - ☐ C. Cannot be determined.

3. Aircraft aluminum skin is easily worked due to these two characteristics _____
    - ☐ A. malleable and ductile.
    - ☐ B. elastic and strong.
    - ☐ C. permeable and hard.

4. The corrosion resistance of titanium landing gear parts would be as good, or better, than stainless steel.
    - ☐ A. True
    - ☐ B. False
    - ☐ C. Cannot be determined.

5. The cast housing of a turbine engine gearbox must be quenched during the heat treatment process. Which of the following solutions has the slowest cooling potential?
    - ☐ A. Oil
    - ☐ B. Water
    - ☐ C. Salt water (brine)

6. A modern unmanned aircraft is constructed entirely of composites. This indicates that the structure is
    _____
    - ☐ A. ferrous, and utilizing aramid fibers.
    - ☐ B. non-metallic and utilizing fibers in a resin matrix.
    - ☐ C. wood.

7. The tensile strength of composite aircraft structures may be _____ that of steel or aluminum.
    - ☐ A. 100 times
    - ☐ B. 1,000 times
    - ☐ C. 4-6 times

8. The landing gear axle nut of a light aircraft is subject to rotation and severe vibration. Which of the following options could be employed to safety the nut?
    - ☐ A. Self-locking nut.
    - ☐ B. No safety required.
    - ☐ C. Safety wire and castle nut.

9. Elongated bolt holes in aircraft structural members may be drilled to the next larger size.
    - ☐ A. Always.
    - ☐ B. Never.
    - ☐ C. With manufacturer's approval.

10. A damaged aluminum wing skin is repaired with copper rivets. This repair is done without consulting the manufacturer of the aircraft. What is one problem this may cause?
    - ☐ A. Dissimilar metal corrosion.
    - ☐ B. Inadequate rivet hole clearance.
    - ☐ C. No problems will be encountered.

Chapter 7, Final Chapter Exam - Aircraft Materials, Hardware, and Processes

Name:_____   Date:_____

PAGE LEFT BLANK INTENTIONALLY

Section A
Study Aid Questions - Fill In The Blanks

1. The latest information on corrosion control can be found in what publication?

2. Metal corrosion is the deterioration of the metal by _____ or _____ attack.

3. Corrosion can occur on the _____ of metal as well as _____ .

4. _____ or _____ vapor containing _____ combines with oxygen to produce the main source of corrosion.

5. Aircraft operating in salt or corrosive environments are much more susceptible to _____ attacks.

6. _____ can cause structural failure.

7. Direct _____ attack is an attack resulting from a direct exposure of a bare surface to _____ liquids or _____ agents.

8. _____ deposits are very corrosive and give particular trouble where _____ , _____ , _____ , and _____ are located down stream from exhaust components.

9. The most practicable means of controlling the corrosion of _____ is the complete _____ of corrosion by mechanical means and restoring coatings.

10. Any corrosion on the surface of a highly stressed steel component is potentially _____ .

11. _____ corrosion is commonly referred to as dissimilar metal corrosion.

12. When two dissimilar metals are in contact with each other and moisture is present, what process occur?

13. What publications should be consulted for information on a material's possible hazards?

14. Active solvents such as _____ , _____ , _____ , and _____ can be harmful or fatal if swallowed.

15. _____ is mixed with solvent emulsion type cleaners for softening heavy preservative coatings.

CLEANING AND CORROSION CONTROL

Section A
True or False

_____ 1. If left unchecked, corrosion can cause eventual structure failure.

_____ 2. Metal corrosion will not weaken the overall structural strength of a component.

_____ 3. During corrosion, metal is converted into a metallic compound such as an oxide, hydroxide, or sulfate.

_____ 4. Metal that is oxidized suffers what may be called arrodic change.

_____ 5. The corrosive agent undergoes arrodic change.

_____ 6. An electrochemical attack may be likened chemically to the electrolytic reaction.

_____ 7. Caustic cleaning solutions in concentrated form are completely safe to use around aircraft.

_____ 8. Very severe intergranular corrosion may cause the surface of the metal to exfoliate.

_____ 9. Dissimilar metal components that come in contact with each other will normally not cause a problem.

_____ 10. Surface corrosion is often caused by an attack along the grain boundaries of an alloy.

Section A
Matching

1. Using the Figure below, match these terms to the proper areas.
   Cathodic   Electron Flow   Current Flow   Anodic

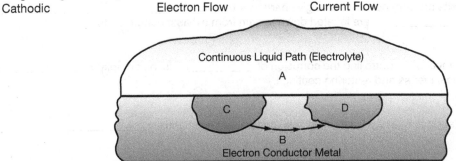

A. _____   C. _____

B. _____   D. _____

2. Using the Figure below, match these terms to the proper areas.
   Intergranular   Corrosion   Anode Paint   Film Cladding   Cathode

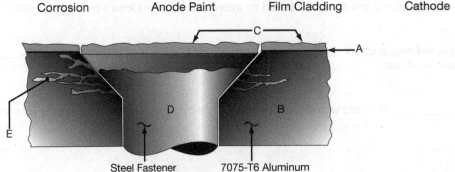

A. _____   C. _____   E. _____

B. _____   D. _____

Match the correct picture with the type of corrosion listed by placing the letter of the picture in the correct blank.

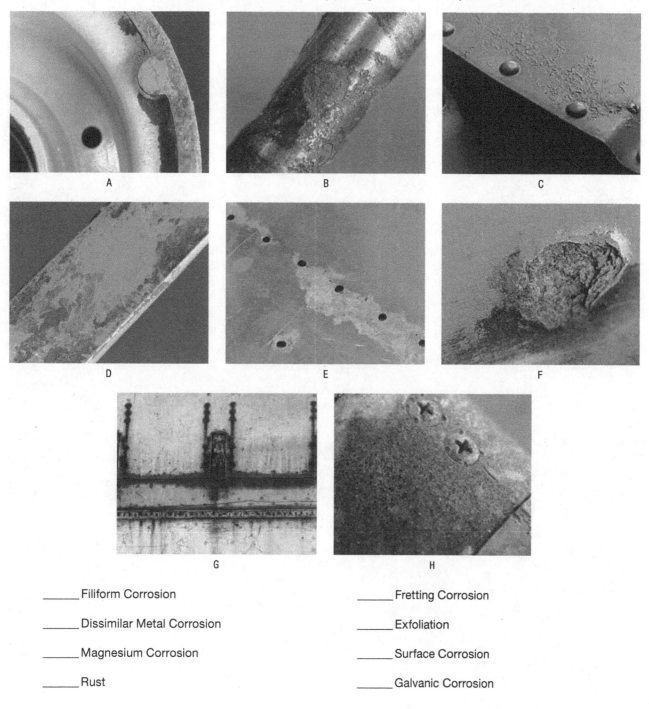

A

B

C

D

E

F

G

H

_____ Filiform Corrosion

_____ Dissimilar Metal Corrosion

_____ Magnesium Corrosion

_____ Rust

_____ Fretting Corrosion

_____ Exfoliation

_____ Surface Corrosion

_____ Galvanic Corrosion

Chapter 8, Section A - Cleaning and Corrosion Control

Name: _____ Date: _____

CLEANING AND CORROSION CONTROL

PAGE LEFT BLANK INTENTIONALLY

Section B
Knowledge Application Questions
Short Answers

1. What is the main source of corrosion in an aircraft?

2. What are the two general classifications of corrosion?

3. Describe direct chemical attack.

4. Describe electrochemical attack.

5. What kind of corrosion can be caused by inducing contamination into a metal's surface by using steel wool on aluminum?

6. What does the form of corrosion depend upon?

7. A form of surface corrosion, filiform corrosion, has what type of appearance?

8. What often causes filiform corrosion?

9. Describe what causes intergranular corrosion.

10. What are the two main factors that affect corrosion?

11. List the areas that are more prone to corrosion on aircraft.

12. List the steps in corrosion removal.

13. Explain the procedure for removing rust on low stressed steel surfaces.

14. How do stronger aluminum alloys that are unpainted prevent surface corrosion?

15. What should be referred to if the surface treatment chemical label does not list all possible hazards associated with a substance?

Section B
Troubleshooting Questions

1. An aircraft operating in or around salt water environments needs extra corrosion inspections and protection. What areas of the aircraft need to be inspected and why?

2. Drain holes are found plugged with material and standing water is found in this area of the aircraft. What should be done?

3. An aircraft has been operating in a salt water environment and several landings have caused the brakes to become very hot upon landing. During your inspection of the wheel well and landing gear what areas and items do you need to pay particular attention during the inspection process?

4. While inspecting an aircraft, you find the control cables have external corrosion. What should be accomplished?

5. During an inspection a component is classified to have negligible corrosion damage. What should be done to this component?

Section B
Exercises

1. Is it acceptable to place aluminum alloy in direct contact with carbon alloy steels?

2. You have been assigned to clean an anodized surface. What can you use to complete this task?

3. The job assignment is to clean an engine using a chemical cleaner or solvent that you are not familiar with. What should you review before doing this task?

4. During an inspection, a structural component requires extensive removal of material to remove corrosion from the part. After removing considerable amounts of material, a decision must be made whether the part can continue in service. Other than the maintenance manual what other resource can you refer to?

5. During a structural repair it is necessary to place two non magnesium dissimilar metals in contact with each other. What should be done to prevent dissimilar metal corrosion between these metals?

Chapter 8, Section B - Cleaning and Corrosion Control

Name:_____   Date:_____

Section C
Final Chapter Exam - Multiple Choice

1. Which of the following are acceptable to use when utilizing chemical cleaning agents on aircraft?
   01. Synthetic fiber wiping cloths when using a flammable agent.
   02. Cotton fiber wiping cloths when using a flammable agent.
   03. Atomizing spray equipment.
   ☐ A. 01 and 03
   ☐ B. 02
   ☐ C. 01

2. When an anodized surface coating is damaged in service, it can be partially restored by _____
   ☐ A. applying a thin coat of zinc chromate primer.
   ☐ B. chemical surface treatment.
   ☐ C. use of a suitable mild cleaner.

3. A primary reason why ordinary or otherwise nonapproved cleaning compounds should not be used when washing aircraft is because their use can result in _____
   ☐ A. hydrogen embrittlement in metal structures.
   ☐ B. hydrogen embrittlement in nonmetallic materials.
   ☐ C. a general inability to remove compound residues.

4. Fayed surfaces cause concern in chemical cleaning because of the danger of _____
   ☐ A. forming passive oxides.
   ☐ B. entrapping corrosive materials.
   ☐ C. corrosion by imbedded iron oxide.

5. Which of these materials is the most cathodic?
   ☐ A. Zinc.
   ☐ B. 2024 aluminum alloy.
   ☐ C. Stainless steel.

6. Why is it important not to rotate the crankshaft after the corrosion preventive mixture has been put into the cylinders on engines prepared for storage?
   ☐ A. Engine damage can occur from hydraulic lock.
   ☐ B. Fuel may be drawn into one or more cylinders and dilute or wash off the corrosion preventive mixture.
   ☐ C. The seal of corrosion preventive mixture will be broken.

7. What should be done to prevent rapid deterioration when oil or grease come in contact with a tire?
   ☐ A. Wipe the tire thoroughly with a dry cloth, and then rinse with clean water.
   ☐ B. Wipe the tire with a dry cloth followed by a washdown and rinse with soap and water.
   ☐ C. Wipe the tire with a cloth dampened with aromatic naphtha and then wipe dry with a clean cloth.

8. A primary cause of intergranular corrosion is _____
   ☐ A. improper heat treatment.
   ☐ B. dissimilar metal contact.
   ☐ C. improper application of primer.

9. One way of obtaining increased resistance to stress corrosion cracking is by _____
   ☐ A. relieving compressive stresses (via heat treatment) on the metal surface.
   ☐ B. creating compressive stresses (via shot peening) on the metal surface.
   ☐ C. producing nonuniform deformation while cold working during the manufacturing process.

10. Spilled mercury on aluminum _____
    ☐ A. greatly increases susceptibility to hydrogen embrittlement.
    ☐ B. may cause impaired corrosion resistance if left in prolonged contact.
    ☐ C. causes rapid and severe corrosion that is very difficult to control.

CLEANING AND CORROSION CONTROL

11. What may be used to remove corrosion from highly stressed steel surfaces?
    - ☐ A. Steel wire brushes.
    - ☐ B. Fine grit aluminum oxide.
    - ☐ C. Medium grit carborundum paper.

12. Fretting corrosion is most likely to occur when _____
    - ☐ A. two surfaces fit tightly together but can move relative to one another
    - ☐ B. only when two dissimilar metals are in contact
    - ☐ C. two surfaces fit loosely together and can move relative to one another

13. Which of the listed conditions is NOT one of the requirements for corrosion to occur?
    - ☐ A. The presence of an electrolyte.
    - ☐ B. Electrical contact between an anodic area and a cathodic area.
    - ☐ C. The presence of a passive oxide film.

14. A nonelectrolytic chemical treatment for aluminum alloys to increase corrosion resistance and paint bonding qualities is called _____
    - ☐ A. anodizing.
    - ☐ B. alodizing.
    - ☐ C. dichromating.

15. Which of the following may not be detectable even by careful visual inspection of the surface of aluminum alloy parts or structures?
    - ☐ A. Filiform corrosion.
    - ☐ B. Intergranular corrosion.
    - ☐ C. Uniform etch corrosion.

FLUID LINES AND FITTINGS

Section A
Study Aid Questions - Fill In The Blanks

1. Metal tubing is sized by the _____ and is measured fractionally in _____ of an inch.

2. Before making repairs to any aircraft tubing, it is important to make _____ of the tubing materials.

3. If a tube bursts or cracks, it is generally the result of _____, _____, or _____.

4. All tubing is pressure tested prior to _____ and is _____ withstand several times operating pressure.

5. Aircraft fluid lines are usually made of _____ or _____.

6. When cutting tubing, it is important to produce a _____ end, free of _____.

7. If a tube cutter is not available, use a _____.

8. Tubing under _____ in diameter usually can be bent without the use of a _____.

9. A new piece of tubing should be cut approximately _____ % longer than the tube to be replaced.

10. Never use an _____ flaring tool which produces a flare of 45 degrees.

11. Standard AN fittings are identified by their _____ or _____ color.

12. _____ is never used in the construction of flexible fluid lines.

13. _____ is a synthetic rubber compound which has an acetylene base.

14. Hose is also designated by a dash number, according to its _____.

15. _____ are identification markings consisting of lines, letters, and numbers that are _____ on the hose.

FLUID LINES AND FITTINGS

_____ 1. All fluid lines must be secured at specified intervals.

_____ 2. Never use bonded clamps to secure metal hydraulic, fuel, or oil lines in place.

_____ 3. Clamps or supporting clips smaller than the outside diameter of the hose may restrict the flow of fluids through the hose.

_____ 4. When needed, a 45 degree flaring tool can be used with aircraft tubing.

_____ 5. Fluid lines in aircraft are often identified by markers, color codes, words, and geometric symbols.

_____ 6. Fuel lines are normally marked using red markings.

_____ 7. Lubrication lines are generally marked using yellow markings.

_____ 8. A flared tube fitting consists of an AN 774 and a nut.

_____ 9. The dash number following the AN number indicates the size of the tubing or hose for which the fitting is made.

_____ 10. The material code letter following the AN number D shows the fitting is made of steel.

_____ 11. A popular repair system for connecting and repairing hydraulic lines on transport category aircraft is the use of Permaswage fittings.

_____ 12. MS flareless fittings cannot be used on aircraft.

_____ 13. Swaged fittings are used to join hydraulic lines in areas where routine disconnections are not required.

_____ 14. It is acceptable practice to pull a line down tight by the use of the B nut.

_____ 15. Never tighten a flareless tube nut beyond one-third turn.

Section A
Matching

Match the bend results in the figure below with the tubes shown below by placing the letter in the blank.

_____ Kinked

_____ Wrinkled

_____ Good

_____ Flattened

Chapter 9, Section A - Fluid Lines and Fittings

Name:_____   Date:_____

1. What are the four processes needed to form tubes?

2. After a tube cutter has been placed into position, which way should it be rotated?

3. After cutting the tubing, the ends of the tubing must be deburred. Explain how this is done.

4. During deburring tubing, what precaution needs to be observed?

5. Explain the basic procedure for flaring a tube.

6. What are the limits with regard to rigid tubing minor dents and scratches?

7. When replacing rigid tubing, the new line's layout should always be checked for what?

8. Hose materials are most commonly made from what type of materials?

9. What three categories are flexible hose classified by?

10. What do lay lines and identification markings consist of?

FLUID LINES AND FITTINGS

1. An aluminum alloy-5 flared fitting tubing nut should be torqued to?

2. What is the MS number of a cross flareless tube fitting?

3. Locate the number for an AN union standard fitting?

4. What color code does an aluminum alloy number of 5052 have?

5. What standard bend radius should a 1" tube have, being bent with a portable hand bender?

6. List the items that are included in the inspection of flexible hoses.

7. After assembly of a flexible hose, what inspection should be accomplished?

8. Explain the procedure to assemble a flexible hose.

9. List the items that should be considered when installing flexible hose.

10. When installing a flexible hose assembly, how much slack does it need? How far apart do hoses need to be supported? How is hose twist determined?

Section C
Final Chapter Exam - Multiple Choice

1. Which of the statements below is true?
   01. Bonded clamps are used for support when installing metal tubing.
   02. Unbonded clamps are used for support when installing wiring.
   ☐ A. Only 01 is true.
   ☐ B. Both 01 and 02 are true.
   ☐ C. Neither 01 nor 02 is true.

2. From the following sequences of steps, indicate the proper order to make a single flare on a piece of tubing:
   01. Place the tube in the proper size hole in the flaring block.
   02. Project the end of the tube slightly from the top of the flaring tool, about the thickness of a dime.
   03. Slip the fitting nut and sleeve on the tube.
   04. Strike the plunger several light blows with a light weight mallet and turn the plunger one half turn after each blow.
   05. Tighten the clamp bar securely to prevent slippage.
   06. Center the plunger or flaring pin over the tube.
   ☐ A. 01, 03, 05, 02, 04, 06
   ☐ B. 03, 01, 06, 02, 05, 04
   ☐ C. 03, 01, 02, 06, 05, 04

3. The primary purpose of providing suitable bends in fluid and pneumatic metal tubing runs is to _____
   ☐ A. clear obstacles and make turns in aircraft structures.
   ☐ B. provide for access within aircraft structures.
   ☐ C. prevent excessive stress on the tubing.

4. Which coupling nut should be selected for use with 1/2-inch aluminum oil lines which are to be assembled using flared tube ends and standard AN nuts, sleeves, and fittings?
   ☐ A. AN-818-16
   ☐ B. AN-818-8
   ☐ C. AN-818-5

5. In most aircraft hydraulic systems, two piece tube connectors consisting of a sleeve and a nut are used when a tubing flare is required. The use of this type connector eliminates _____
   ☐ A. the flaring operation prior to assembly.
   ☐ B. the possibility of reducing the flare thickness by wiping or ironing during the tightening process.
   ☐ C. wrench damage to the tubing during the tightening process.

6. Which of the following statements is/are correct in reference to flare fittings?
   01. AN fittings have an identifying shoulder between the end of the threads and the flare cone.
   02. AC and AN fittings are considered identical except for material composition and identifying colors.
   03. AN fittings are generally interchangeable with AC fittings of compatible material composition.
   ☐ A. 01
   ☐ B. 01 and 03
   ☐ C. 01, 02, and 03

7. Which tubing's have the characteristics (high strength, abrasion resistance) necessary for use in a high pressure (3,000 psi) hydraulic system for operation of landing gear and flaps?
   ☐ A. 2024-T or 5052-0 aluminum alloy.
   ☐ B. Corrosion resistant steel annealed or 1/4H.
   ☐ C. 1100-1/2H or 3003-1/2H aluminum alloy.

8. Flexible hose used in aircraft systems is classified in size according to _____
   ☐ A. outside diameter.
   ☐ B. wall thickness.
   ☐ C. inside diameter.

FLUID LINES AND FITTINGS

9. The material specifications for a certain aircraft require that a replacement oil line be fabricated from 3/4-inch 0.072 5052-0 aluminum alloy tubing. What is the inside dimension of this tubing?
   - ☐ A. 0.606 inch
   - ☐ B. 0.688 inch
   - ☐ C. 0.750 inch

10. A gas or fluid line marked with the letters PHDAN is _____
   - ☐ A. a dual-purpose pneumatic and/or hydraulic line for normal and emergency system use.
   - ☐ B. used to carry a hazardous substance.
   - ☐ C. a pneumatic or hydraulic system drain or discharge line.

11. In a metal tubing installation _____
   - ☐ A. rigid straight line runs are preferable.
   - ☐ B. tension is undesirable because pressurization will cause it to expand and shift.
   - ☐ C. a tube may be pulled in line if the nut will start on the threaded coupling.

12. Flexible lines must be installed with _____
   - ☐ A. enough slack to allow maximum flexing during operation.
   - ☐ B. a slack of at least 10 to 12 percent of the length.
   - ☐ C. a slack of 5 to 8 percent of the length.

13. Which statement is true regarding the variety of symbols utilized on the identifying color-code bands that are currently used on aircraft plumbing lines?
   - ☐ A. Symbols are composed of various single colors according to line content.
   - ☐ B. Symbols are always black against a white background regardless of line content.
   - ☐ C. Symbols are composed of one to three contrasting colors according to line content.

14. The best tool to use when cutting aluminum tubing, or any tubing of moderately soft metal is a _____
   - ☐ A. hand operated wheel-type tubing cutter.
   - ☐ B. fine-tooth hacksaw.
   - ☐ C. circular-saw equipped with an abrasive cutting wheel.

15. A scratch or nick in aluminum tubing can be repaired provided it does not _____
   - ☐ A. appear in the heel of a bend.
   - ☐ B. appear on the inside of a bend.
   - ☐ C. exceed 10 percent of the tube OD on a straight section.

16. Hydraulic tubing, which is damaged in a localized area to such an extent that repair is necessary, may be repaired _____
   - ☐ A. by cutting out the damaged area and utilizing a swaged tube fitting to join the tube ends.
   - ☐ B. only by replacing the tubing section run (connection to connection) using the same size and material as the original.
   - ☐ C. by cutting out the damaged section and soldering in a replacement section of tubing.

17. The term "cold flow" is generally associated with _____
   - ☐ A. the effects of low temperature gasses or liquids flowing in hose or tubing.
   - ☐ B. impressions left in natural or synthetic rubber hose material.
   - ☐ C. flexibility characteristics of various hose materials at low ambient temperatures.

Section A
Study Aid Questions - Multiple Choice, True or False

1. A thorough inspection will involve _____ the aircraft.
   - ☐ A. cleaning
   - ☐ B. servicing
   - ☐ C. fueling

2. A _____ must be used to perform all aircraft inspections.
   - ☐ A. power washer
   - ☐ B. set of scales
   - ☐ C. checklist

3. The checklist used to inspect a particular aircraft must be FAA approved and published.
   - ☐ A. True
   - ☐ B. False
   - ☐ C. Cannot be determined.

4. The aircraft maintenance manual is commonly used for overhaul of specific aircraft components.
   - ☐ A. True
   - ☐ B. False
   - ☐ C. Cannot be determined.

5. The _____ is used to thoroughly service a component after it is removed from an aircraft.
   - ☐ A. maintenance manual
   - ☐ B. pilots operating handbook
   - ☐ C. overhaul manual

6. Airspeed limitations for a specific aircraft would be found in the _____
   - ☐ A. TCDS.
   - ☐ B. overhaul manual.
   - ☐ C. component assembly instructions.

7. A typical preflight inspection is performed by _____ and would include _____
   - ☐ A. the pilot, fuel draining
   - ☐ B. the pilot, walking around the aircraft
   - ☐ C. the mechanic, walking around the aircraft

8. A 100 hour inspection of an aircraft may be performed, and returned to service, by _____
   - ☐ A. a certified airframe and powerplant mechanic.
   - ☐ B. a certified repair technician.
   - ☐ C. a designated supervisor.

9. An annual aircraft inspection requires an airframe and powerplant mechanic with _____ to return the aircraft to service.
   - ☐ A. inspection authorization
   - ☐ B. inspection approval
   - ☐ C. inspection endorsement

10. Progressive inspections are desirable to minimize aircraft down time during the inspection.
    - ☐ A. True
    - ☐ B. False
    - ☐ C. Cannot be determined.

11. _____ are progressive inspections designed for larger turbine powered aircraft.
    - ☐ A. Constant inspections
    - ☐ B. Intermittent inspections
    - ☐ C. Continuous inspections

INSPECTION CONCEPTS AND TECHNIQUES

12. _____ has standardized the format of aircraft maintenance manuals for ease in locating information.
   ☐ A. ISTEP
   ☐ B. ATA iSpec 2200
   ☐ C. Astep

13. A special inspection may include the following _____
   ☐ A. overweight landing, lightning strike, fuel contamination.
   ☐ B. fire damage, lightning strike, overweight landing.
   ☐ C. seaplane, helicopter, powered parachute.

14. _____ merit special inspections of aerial application aircraft.
   ☐ A. Careless assembly processes
   ☐ B. Poor maintenance practices
   ☐ C. Susceptibility to corrosion and flight profiles

15. Inserting a camera into an area inaccessible to direct visual inspection is a form of _____
   ☐ A. magnetic particle inspection.
   ☐ B. liquid penetrant inspection.
   ☐ C. borescope inspection.

16. _____ inspections are limited to surface crack detection in aircraft parts.
   ☐ A. Eddy current
   ☐ B. Ultrasonic
   ☐ C. Liquid penetrant

17. An indication is a defect detected by the disrupted magnetic field during a magnetic particle inspection.
   ☐ A. True
   ☐ B. False
   ☐ C. Cannot be determined.

18. The orientation of the magnetic field during a magnetic particle inspection may include _____
   ☐ A. circular and longitudinal.
   ☐ B. lateral and longitudinal.
   ☐ C. vertical and horizontal.

19. Another common name for radiographic inspection is _____
   ☐ A. varga ray
   ☐ B. visual
   ☐ C. x-ray

20. A solid, or structurally sound, composite aircraft part will produce a _____ when tapped with a coin.
   ☐ A. ring
   ☐ B. dull thud
   ☐ C. high pitched whine

Section B
Knowledge Application Questions
Short Answers

1. If you are the maintenance planner for a fleet of large, turbine powered aircraft, what type of inspection program would be most desirable for you to request approval from the FAA?

2. Hydraulic lines should be inspected for what condition?

3. Who must you be in order to supervise or conduct a progressive inspection?

4. What is the inspection interval for aircraft altimeters and transponders if operated in IFR conditions?

5. What classification of turbulence would require an over "G" inspection?

6. Are composite or metallic aircraft more likely to have damage from a lightning strike?

7. Seaplane operation would require careful inspections for what types of damage?

8. What type of inspection is best used to determine aluminum hardness after fire damage?

9. What is one precaution that must be observed when using radiographic inspection methods?

10. An aircraft weld should possess what common characteristics?

Chapter 10, Section B - Inspection Concepts and Techniques

Name:_____ Date:_____

PAGE LEFT BLANK INTENTIONALLY

Section C
Final Chapter Exam - Multiple Choice, True or False

1. Aircraft inspection checklists must be FAA approved.
   - ☐ A. True
   - ☐ B. False
   - ☐ C. Cannot be determined.

2. A 100 inspection would not include the engine controls.
   - ☐ A. True
   - ☐ B. False
   - ☐ C. Cannot be determined.

3. Removing an aircraft cowl and inspection access plates are not part of a routine annual inspection.
   - ☐ A. True
   - ☐ B. False
   - ☐ C. Cannot be determined.

4. An aircraft engine overhaul manual is commonly used for routine inspections and service.
   - ☐ A. True
   - ☐ B. False
   - ☐ C. Cannot be determined.

5. Service bulletins are FAA publications and must be complied with in all cases.
   - ☐ A. True
   - ☐ B. False
   - ☐ C. Cannot be determined.

6. A preflight inspection differs from a progressive inspection as to the size of the aircraft.
   - ☐ A. True
   - ☐ B. False
   - ☐ C. Cannot be determined.

7. Primary and secondary structures are covered in the aircraft Structural Repair Manual.
   - ☐ A. True
   - ☐ B. False
   - ☐ C. Cannot be determined.

8. A Type Certificate Data Sheet is useful for aircraft inspections as it contains specific information about an aircraft.
   - ☐ A. True
   - ☐ B. False
   - ☐ C. Cannot be determined.

9. A special flight permit is issued by the FAA for the purpose of operating an aircraft that is technically unairworthy, but remains safe for limited flight.
   - ☐ A. True
   - ☐ B. False
   - ☐ C. Cannot be determined.

10. Liquid penetrant inspections require cleaning of the part before the inspection.
    - ☐ A. True
    - ☐ B. False
    - ☐ C. Cannot be determined.

Chapter 10, Final Chapter Exam - Inspection Concepts and Techniques

Name:_____   Date:_____

PAGE LEFT BLANK INTENTIONALLY

Section A
Study Aid Questions - Fill In The Blanks

1. Metal head hammers are usually sized according to the _____ of the head.

2. Soft-faced hammers are used for striking _____ that are easily _____.

3. Soft-faced hammers can be made of _____, _____, _____, _____, _____, or _____.

4. Always strike the work squarely with the _____ of the hammer.

5. A common screwdriver must fill at least _____ of the screw slot.

6. Two types of recessed head screws in common use are the _____ and the _____.

7. The pliers used most frequently in aircraft work are the _____, _____, and _____.

8. The size of pliers is indicated by their overall _____.

9. Large indentations in metal, used to start a twist drill are made using a _____.

10. _____ wrenches are popular tools because of their usefulness in close quarters.

11. One option for removing a nut from a bolt is the _____.

HAND TOOLS AND MEASURING DEVICES

12. When nuts must be removed from studs or bolts that are difficult to access, a _____ can be used.

13. When a definite amount of pressure or torque must be applied to a bolt, a _____ should be used.

14. Commonly used torque wrenches include the _____ , _____ , _____ , and _____ types.

15. Aviation snips are designed for cutting heat-treated _____ and _____ .

Section A
True or False

_____ 1.   The pitch of the blade of a hacksaw indicates the number of teeth per inch.

_____ 2.   A hacksaw blade with 32 teeth per inch should be used when cutting machine steel.

_____ 3.   Use a 32 teeth per inch hacksaw blade for cutting thin-walled tubing and sheet metal.

_____ 4.   Chisels are usually made of eight-sided tool steel bar stock.

_____ 5.   The size of a flat cold chisel is determined by the width of the cutting edge.

_____ 6.   The part of a file that fits the handle is called the point.

_____ 7.   Flat files are slightly wider toward the point in both width and thickness.

_____ 8.   Draw filing is grasping it at each end, crosswise to the work, then moving it lengthwise with the work.

_____ 9.   Hard metal particles lodged in the teeth of the file can be removed by using a file card or wire brush.

_____ 10. The principle parts of a twist drill are the shank, the body, and the head.

_____ 11. The diameter of a twist drill may be given in one of three ways (1) fractions, (2) letters, (3) numbers.

_____ 12. Lip angle of a normal drill bit is generally 15 degrees.

_____ 13. A tap is used to cut threads on the inside of a hole.

_____ 14. A die is used to cut threads on the inside of a hole.

_____ 15. Solid dies are not adjustable.

Section B
Matching

Use the drawing below to identify the component parts of a micrometer.

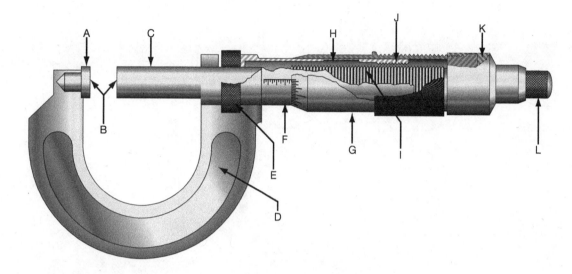

A. _____   D. _____   G. _____   J. _____

B. _____   E. _____   H. _____   K. _____

C. _____   F. _____   I. _____   L. _____

PAGE LEFT BLANK INTENTIONALLY

Section B
Short Answers

1. List the two important rules for using pliers.

2. What is the basic purpose for a drive punch (tapered punch)?

3. What kind of attention do torque wrenches require?

4. What is the main use of round or rat-tail files?

5. List the principle parts of a twist drill.

6. What is the maximum cut for a reamer?

7. What is the purpose of bottoming tap?

8. What is the basic purpose of a counter sink?

9. What are the fixed and movable parts of a micrometer?

10. Slide calipers can be used to measure what types of dimensions?

Section B
Short Answers, Matching

1. A component part needs to be moved over but it has a finished surface. What type of hammer should you use?

2. A screw needs removing and there is limited space above the head. What type of screw driver should you use?

3. A hole needs to be drilled but before drilling, what should be used to prevent the drill bit from wandering on the surface to be drilled?

HAND TOOLS AND MEASURING DEVICES

4. A tight hex nut needs to be removed. What should be used to break it loose?

5. An engine crankcase needs to be tightened down using a definite pressure on the nuts and bolts. What should you use?

6. Some 4130 tubing needs to be cut to certain lengths. What type of hand saw and type of blade should be used?

7. What is the decimal equivalent of a number 30 drill bit?

8. After removing a bolt, the threads in the bolt hole seem to be rusted and have caused it to be difficult to screw in the bolt. What can be done to clean up these threads?

9. A hole needs to be tapped out with 10-32 threads. What size tap drill do you need?

10. A hole 3/8 – 16 needs to be drilled and threaded. What tap drill size would be needed?

11. A 7/16 hole needs to be drilled in mild steel. What is the correct drill speed?

12. Read the micrometer readings A-D below and record your answers.

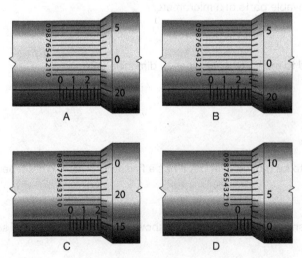

A. _____   B. _____   C. _____   D. _____

Section C
Final Chapter Exam - Multiple Choice

1. Which tool can be used to measure the alignment of a rotor shaft or the plane of rotation of a disk?
   ☐ A. Dial indicator.
   ☐ B. Shaft gauge.
   ☐ C. Protractor.

2. The side clearances of piston rings are measured with _____
   ☐ A. micrometer caliper gauge.
   ☐ B. thickness gauge.
   ☐ C. dial gauge.

3. Which number represents the vernier scale graduation of a micrometer?
   ☐ A. .00001
   ☐ B. .001
   ☐ C. .0001

4. What does the micrometer below read?

   ☐ A. 0.2974
   ☐ B. 0.2792
   ☐ C. 0.3108

5. The measurement reading on the micrometer below is _____.

   ☐ A. 0.2758
   ☐ B. 0.2702
   ☐ C. 0.2851

6. What precision measuring tool is used for measuring crankpin and main bearing journals for out of round wear?
   ☐ A. Dial gauge.
   ☐ B. Micrometer caliper.
   ☐ C. Depth gauge.

7. How can the dimensional inspection of a bearing in a rocker arm be accomplished?
   ☐ A. Depth gauge and micrometer.
   ☐ B. Thickness gauge and push-fit arbor.
   ☐ C. Telescopic gauge and micrometer.

8. What may be used to check the stem on a poppet-type valve for stretch?
   ☐ A. Dial indicator
   ☐ B. Micrometer
   ☐ C. Telescoping gauge

9. What tool is generally used to set a divider to an exact dimension?
   ☐ A. Machinist scale.
   ☐ B. Surface gauge.
   ☐ C. Dial indicator.

10. What tool is generally used to calibrate a micrometer or check its accuracy?
    ☐ A. Gauge block.
    ☐ B. Dial indicator.
    ☐ C. Machinist scale.

Chapter 11, Final Chapter Exam - Hand Tools and Measuring Devices

Name:_____ Date:_____

PAGE LEFT BLANK INTENTIONALLY

Section A
Study Aid Questions - Multiple Choice, True or False

1. The basic parts of an atom include _____
   - ☐ A. electrons, protons, neutrons.
   - ☐ B. electrons, nucleus, orbit.
   - ☐ C. electrons, orbit, space.

2. The smallest particle of any element is referred to as _____
   - ☐ A. an atom.
   - ☐ B. a proton.
   - ☐ C. a molecule.

3. Static electricity is the build up of an electrical charge on an aircraft or other surface.
   - ☐ A. True
   - ☐ B. False
   - ☐ C. Cannot be determined.

4. Two precautions to be observed, when working with aircraft electrical components would be _____
   - ☐ A. do not pry components from a circuit board, heat of soldering should be minimized.
   - ☐ B. heat of soldering should maximized, polarity should be reversed.
   - ☐ C. polarity should be reversed, power should be left on the circuit during repair.

5. _____ and _____ can damage a magnet.
   - ☐ A. Heat, silicone
   - ☐ B. Silicone, water
   - ☐ C. Heat, impact

6. The magnetic properties of copper wire create electromagnetism.
   - ☐ A. True
   - ☐ B. False
   - ☐ C. Cannot be determined.

7. Magnetism around a conductor _____ when the applied current is stopped.
   - ☐ A. increases
   - ☐ B. decreases
   - ☐ C. stops

8. Reversing the current in an electromagnet also reverses the _____
   - ☐ A. voltage.
   - ☐ B. inductance.
   - ☐ C. polarity.

9. Ohm's law is useful for determining _____
   - ☐ A. relationships between power, conductor area, and mass.
   - ☐ B. relationships between power, voltage, and applied voltage.
   - ☐ C. relationships between voltage, amperage, and resistance.

10. Wire conductors _____ in resistance as temperature increases.
    - ☐ A. increase
    - ☐ B. decrease
    - ☐ C. stay the same

11. The production of an electrical signal through mechanical strain is referred to as _____
    - ☐ A. stress.
    - ☐ B. power.
    - ☐ C. piezoelectrics.

12. Electronic symbols are commonly found on _____
    ☐ A. wire code tags.
    ☐ B. aircraft panel doors.
    ☐ C. schematics.

13. A resistor will _____ current in a circuit and may be fixed or variable.
    ☐ A. oppose
    ☐ B. promote
    ☐ C. create

14. Two types of circuit protective devices would include _____
    ☐ A. fuses, circuit breakers.
    ☐ B. conductor, resistor.
    ☐ C. thermal protectors, battery.

15. A DPDT switch would also be referred to as a _____ switch.
    ☐ A. single pole, double throw
    ☐ B. double pole double throw
    ☐ C. double pole, single throw

16. DC circuits can be classified as _____ and _____
    ☐ A. voltage, current.
    ☐ B. series, parallel.
    ☐ C. resistance, inductance.

17. The effective value of alternating current is referred to as RMA and is a mathematic calculation based on .707 as a constant.
    ☐ A. True
    ☐ B. False
    ☐ C. Cannot be determined.

18. A capacitor serves as a _____ in an electrical circuit.
    ☐ A. resistance
    ☐ B. inductance
    ☐ C. reservoir

19. When a conductor is passed through an electromagnetic field, this is referred to as _____
    ☐ A. impedance.
    ☐ B. inductance.
    ☐ C. resistance.

20. To convert 110 volts AC to 12 volts AC for use in an aircraft, a _____ is used.
    ☐ A. transformer
    ☐ B. inverter
    ☐ C. voltage resistor

21. An ohmmeter measures _____ and requires that power be applied to the circuit.
    ☐ A. resistance
    ☐ B. voltage
    ☐ C. amperage

22. Aircraft electrical troubleshooting is commonly the identification of a circuit that contains a short, or an open, that is unintentional.
    ☐ A. True
    ☐ B. False
    ☐ C. Cannot be determined.

23. A secondary cell battery would be one that is not rechargeable.
    - ☐ A. True
    - ☐ B. False
    - ☐ C. Cannot be determined.

24. A lead acid battery measures _____ volts per cell.
    - ☐ A. two
    - ☐ B. one
    - ☐ C. six

25. Battery voltage is determined by the number of cells connected in _____
    - ☐ A. parallel.
    - ☐ B. series.
    - ☐ C. series/parallel.

26. A transistor is a three terminal device that is used to amplify signals and control current in aircraft electrical circuits.
    - ☐ A. True ·
    - ☐ B. False
    - ☐ C. Cannot be determined.

27. In considering logic circuits, several propositions, when combined, will form a _____
    - ☐ A. logical conclusion.
    - ☐ B. logical function.
    - ☐ C. logical determination.

28. The armature of a DC generator rotates within the _____
    - ☐ A. field coils of the field frame.
    - ☐ B. field coils of the armature frame.
    - ☐ C. field coils of the brush assembly.

29. A split phase electrical motor is of the _____ type.
    - ☐ A. alternator
    - ☐ B. generator
    - ☐ C. self starting

30. A GCU, or Generator Control Unit, senses the voltage in a large aircraft electrical circuit and adjust it to preset values.
    - ☐ A. True
    - ☐ B. False
    - ☐ C. Cannot be determined.

PAGE LEFT BLANK INTENTIONALLY

FUNDAMENTALS OF ELECTRICITY AND ELECTRONICS

Section B
Knowledge Application Questions
Short Answers

1. When two magnets are brought together, which poles will attract each other?

2. A series DC aircraft electrical circuit has a 12 volt battery, a 10 ohm resistor, and a 2 ohm resistor. What is the current flow in this circuit?

3. A series DC aircraft electrical circuit contains a 3 ohm resistor, a 5 ohm resistor, and is carrying 10 amps. What is the voltage in the circuit?

4. A parallel DC aircraft electrical circuit has a 24 volt battery, a 2 ohm resistance, and a 16 ohm resistance. What is the current flow in this circuit?

5. An aircraft technician wishes to install an additional landing light onto a light aircraft for use in unimproved airport landings. What are the minimum components required for this installation to function safely?

6. What would the watts of power be for a DC aircraft flap circuit that had a 10 ohm resistor, a 12 ohm resistor, and a 3 ohm resistor in series with a 12 volt battery?

7. A resistor in an aircraft dome light circuit breaks loose and is damaged. The old resistor has a red band, brown band, then a black band. What is the rated resistance of this component to determine a satisfactory replacement?

8. A twelve cell lead acid battery would produce how many volts?

9. A large aircraft has a series AC circuit to operate the landing gear position lights on the instrument panel. The circuit contains 12 ohms of resistance and is 110 volts. How much current will flow in this system?

10. An aircraft transformer contains 4 turns of wire in the primary and 16 turns of wire in the secondary. A voltage of 12 volts is applied to the primary coil. What is the secondary output voltage?

FUNDAMENTALS OF ELECTRICITY AND ELECTRONICS

PAGE LEFT BLANK INTENTIONALLY

FUNDAMENTALS OF ELECTRICITY AND ELECTRONICS

Section C
Final Chapter Exam - Multiple Choice, True or False

1. A molecule is made up of multiple _____
   - ☐ A. neutrons.
   - ☐ B. protons.
   - ☐ C. atoms.

2. The process of cutting lines of magnetic flux with a conductor, and generating voltage, is the basis of alternator and generator operation.
   - ☐ A. True
   - ☐ B. False
   - ☐ C. Cannot be determined.

3. Electromotive force is another way of describing _____
   - ☐ A. amperage.
   - ☐ B. voltage.
   - ☐ C. resistance.

4. The flow of electricity is not fully understood and has been presented as both conventional flow and electron flow theories.
   - ☐ A. True
   - ☐ B. False
   - ☐ C. Cannot be determined.

5. Resistance in a series DC circuit is _____
   - ☐ A. the sum of the resistors values.
   - ☐ B. the product of the resistors values.
   - ☐ C. Cannot be determined.

6. Resistance in a parallel DC circuit is _____
   - ☐ A. always more than the lowest resistance value.
   - ☐ B. always less than the lowest resistance value.
   - ☐ C. Cannot be determined.

7. A capacitor acts as a gate to allow current flow in one direction only.
   - ☐ A. True
   - ☐ B. False
   - ☐ C. Cannot be determined.

8. Inductance requires a coil of wire, a conductor, a completed circuit, and _____
   - ☐ A. capacitance.
   - ☐ B. reactance.
   - ☐ C. movement.

9. When using a multimeter, the circuit to be tested for resistance must be _____
   - ☐ A. open.
   - ☐ B. isolated.
   - ☐ C. receiving system power.

10. Lead acid aircraft batteries are best tested _____
    - ☐ A. with a multimeter.
    - ☐ B. with a hydrometer.
    - ☐ C. cannot be tested.

Chapter 12, Final Chapter Exam - Fundamentals of Electricity and Electronics

Name:_____   Date:_____

FUNDAMENTALS OF ELECTRICITY AND ELECTRONICS

PAGE LEFT BLANK INTENTIONALLY

MECHANIC PRIVILEGES AND LIMITATIONS

Section A
Study Aid Questions - Multiple Choice, True or False

1. 14 CFR Part 65 relates to the certification of airmen other than _____ crew members.
    - ☐ A. maintenance
    - ☐ B. union
    - ☐ C. flight

2. The mechanic, and the repairman certificates are considered to be different classifications by the FAA.
    - ☐ A. True
    - ☐ B. False
    - ☐ C. Cannot be determined.

3. The primary difference between the mechanic certificate and the repairman certificate is that the mechanic can perform more difficult repairs than the repairman.
    - ☐ A. True
    - ☐ B. False
    - ☐ C. Cannot be determined.

4. A conviction, for the sale of marijuana, may result in your mechanic certificate being suspended or revoked.
    - ☐ A. True
    - ☐ B. False
    - ☐ C. Cannot be determined.

5. If you _____ your mechanic certificate, this means you return it voluntarily.
    - ☐ A. revoke
    - ☐ B. suspend
    - ☐ C. surrender

6. The mechanic certificate must be renewed each year or it will expire.
    - ☐ A. True
    - ☐ B. False
    - ☐ C. Cannot be determined.

7. The two methods by which an applicant for a mechanics certificate may retake a failed written test include _____ and _____.
    - ☐ A. waiting 30 days, obtain a waiver from the FAA.
    - ☐ B. waiting 60 days, receive additional instruction.
    - ☐ C. waiting 30 days, receive additional instruction with a signed statement.

8. A mistake in recording the part number, of a part installed on an aircraft, if unintentional, is cause for revoking a mechanics certificate.
    - ☐ A. True
    - ☐ B. False
    - ☐ C. Cannot be determined.

9. The FAA must be notified within _____ days of a change of address of any person holding a mechanic certificate.
    - ☐ A. 30
    - ☐ B. 60
    - ☐ C. 90

10. Refusing to submit to drug and alcohol testing is _____
    - ☐ A. allowed if the mechanic obtains a waiver.
    - ☐ B. encouraged as it infringes upon a mechanics civil rights.
    - ☐ C. grounds for revoking their certificate.

MECHANIC PRIVILEGES AND LIMITATIONS

11. A certified mechanic must be at least _____ years of age.
    ☐ A. 18
    ☐ B. 16
    ☐ C. 14

12. The mechanic ratings include _____ and _____
    ☐ A. general, airframe.
    ☐ B. airframe, powerplant.
    ☐ C. general, powerplant.

13. Propeller knowledge and testing would be included in what rating?
    ☐ A. Powerplant
    ☐ B. Airframe
    ☐ C. General

14. Repairing an altimeter is a privilege of the airframe mechanic.
    ☐ A. True
    ☐ B. False
    ☐ C. Cannot be determined.

15. The recent experience requirements of the mechanics certificate may be fulfilled through supervising maintenance or alteration of aircraft.
    ☐ A. True
    ☐ B. False
    ☐ C. Cannot be determined.

16. A powerplant mechanic may perform a major repair to an aircraft engine but a _____ is required to return it to service.
    ☐ A. waiver
    ☐ B. release
    ☐ C. Inspection Authorization (IA)

17. An airframe and powerplant mechanic may perform, and return to service, a 100 hour inspection on an aircraft, propeller, and engine.
    ☐ A. True
    ☐ B. False
    ☐ C. Cannot be determined.

18. Which of these is required to apply for an inspection authorization certificate?
    ☐ A. An A&P certificate has been held for 3 years.
    ☐ B. You are at least 21 years of age.
    ☐ C. A letter of recommendation from a current IA certificate holder.

19. What is the primary benefit of a mechanic's certificate over a repairman's certificate?
    ☐ A. A repairman's certificate is limited to a specific model aircraft.
    ☐ B. A repairman's certificate is limited to a specific employer or location.
    ☐ C. A repairman's certificate must be renewed every year.

20. A mechanic must exercise good judgment and decision making. This is _____
    ☐ A. professionalism.
    ☐ B. ethics.
    ☐ C. both A and B.

Section B
Knowledge Application Questions
Short Answers

1. A mechanic applicant takes, and passes, all required tests for her rating at age 16. How long must the applicant wait before being granted a mechanics certificate?

2. A mechanic has lived, and worked, in Phoenix, Arizona for 2 years. He is promoted and moves to Mesa, Arizona. When must he notify the FAA of this change?

3. A mechanic receives his certificate in January of 2010. He is asked to serve overseas until April 2015. Is his mechanic certificate still valid upon his return to the US?

4. A mechanic has worked for the airlines for 2 years. She is arrested and charged with driving while intoxicated, but never convicted. What effect will this have on her certificate?

5. An aircraft is modified to include spoilers for rapid descent from altitude. This is a major alteration to the wing structure. Can an airframe and powerplant mechanic perform this work and return it to service?

6. A repairman works for an airline in South Dakota. He quits this job to move to a warmer climate and finds a job in Florida. Does his repairman certificate automatically transfer to his new place of employment?

7. A mechanic writes a logbook entry for a wheel assembly and is asked by the owner to state the wheel was replaced, when in fact, it was repaired. The mechanic states the wheel was replaced. Can the mechanic lose his license for this logbook entry?

8. A mechanic receives a temporary mechanic certificate from the FAA and has a mechanic job the next day. Can this mechanic exercise the privileges of his rating using only the temporary certificate?

9. A mechanic removes an airspeed indicator and sees an obvious defect in the instrument. She repairs the defect and reinstalls the instrument without making a logbook entry. Can the mechanic lose her license for this activity?

10. A mechanic, with Inspection Authorization, repairs a wing skin damaged in an accident. The repair is done according to the structural repair manual and submitted to the FAA on a form 337. Can this mechanic complete the return this aircraft to service after this repair?

Chapter 13, Section B - Mechanic Privileges and Limitations

Name:_____ Date:_____

PAGE LEFT BLANK INTENTIONALLY

Section C
Final Chapter Exam - Multiple Choice, True or False

1. A mechanic must hold their license for _____ years to be eligible for an Inspection Authorization.
   - ☐ A. 5
   - ☐ B. 3
   - ☐ C. 2

2. The FAA requires a fixed base of operation for an Inspection Authorization to be approved.
   - ☐ A. True
   - ☐ B. False
   - ☐ C. Cannot be determined.

3. Falsely reproducing aircraft records can result in _____
   - ☐ A. revocation of your A&P certificate.
   - ☐ B. mandatory drug and alcohol testing.
   - ☐ C. reduction of your mechanic's certificate to a repairman's certificate.

4. What is the minimum passing grade on all FAA exams?
   - ☐ A. 85%
   - ☐ B. 65%
   - ☐ C. 70%

5. Cheating on an FAA exam may be tolerated if certain requirements are met and the FAA administrator is familiar with your limitations.
   - ☐ A. True
   - ☐ B. False
   - ☐ C. Cannot be determined.

6. A security threat, as defined by the TSA, will result in your mechanic application being _____
   - ☐ A. held.
   - ☐ B. revised.
   - ☐ C. submitted.

7. A _____ may request to see your mechanic certificate at your place of employment, while working on aircraft.
   - ☐ A. local police officer
   - ☐ B. NTSB representative
   - ☐ C. Both of the above.

8. A mechanic school student may take the required FAA exams prior to graduation from that school.
   - ☐ A. True
   - ☐ B. False
   - ☐ C. Cannot be determined.

9. _____ months of practical experience, working on aircraft, are required to apply for the airframe and powerplant certificate, if the applicant has not attended a certified school.
   - ☐ A. 24
   - ☐ B. 60
   - ☐ C. 30

10. The application form, to become a certified mechanic, is Form _____.
    - ☐ A. 337
    - ☐ B. 1019-1
    - ☐ C. 8610-2

Chapter 13, Final Chapter Exam - Mechanic Privileges and Limitations

Name:_____ Date:_____

PAGE LEFT BLANK INTENTIONALLY

Section A
Study Aid Questions - Fill in the Blanks

1. Human factors is composed of 10 distinct disciplines. For of the disciplines are _____,

   _____, _____, and _____.

2. _____ awareness can lead to improved quality, an environment that ensures continuing

   worker and aircraft safety and a more involved and responsible work force.

3. _____ is the study of basic behavioral processes.

4. The four elements that make up the PEAR Model are _____,

   _____, _____, _____.

5. The four components of the SHEL Model are _____, _____,

   _____, and _____.

6. _____ includes the study and application of psychology for the purpose of understanding,

   preventing, and relieving psychologically-based distress or dysfunction and to promote subjective well-being and

   personal development.

7. _____ includes the study of a variety of basic behavioral processes, often in a

   laboratory environment.

8. _____ is the study of the dimensions and abilities of the human body. This is essential to

   aviation maintenance due to the environment and space that AMT's have to work in.

9. _____ assures that a life-critical system behaves as needed even when the

   component fails.

HUMAN FACTORS

10. _____ is the interdisciplinary scientific study of minds as information processors.

11. _____ are concerned with relations between people and work.

12. _____ study how people learn and design the methods and materials used to educate people of all ages.

13. An _____ error is an activity that causes an obvious event.

14. An _____ is considered a violation.

15. An _____ error is defined as a human action with unintended consequences.

Section A
True or False

_____ 1. An unintentional error is an unintentional wandering or deviation from accuracy.

_____ 2. In aviation maintenance, an intentional error should really be considered a violation.

_____ 3. A latent error is the specific individual activity that is an obvious event.

_____ 4. An active error is the company issues that lead up to the event.

_____ 5. Lack of communication is a key human factor that can result in suboptimal, incorrect, or faulty maintenance.

_____ 6. A common scenario where communication is critical and a lack thereof can cause problems, is during shift change in an airline or fixed base operator (FBO) operation.

_____ 7. It is vital that work not be continued on a project without both oral and written communication between the technician who started the job and the technician continuing it.

_____ 8. Work should always be done in accordance with the approved procedure and all of the performed steps should bear the signature of the pilot who supervises the work.

_____ 9. Complacency is a human factor in aviation maintenance that typically develops quickly in technicians that are overconfident.

_____ 10. When a technician finds him or herself performing work without documentation, or documenting work that was not performed, it is a sign that complacency may exist.

_____ 11. The technician primarily deals with the physical aspect of the aircraft and its airworthiness.

_____ 12. A fatigued person may also raise his or her standards.

_____ 13. Tiredness is a symptom of fatigue.

_____ 14. Good restful sleep, free from drugs or alcohol is a human necessity to prevent fatigue.

_____ 15. The best remedy for fatigue is to get enough sleep on a regular basis.

Chapter 14, Section A - Human Factors

Name:_____ Date:_____

PAGE LEFT BLANK INTENTIONALLY

Section B
Knowledge Application Questions
Short Answers

1. An aircraft maintenance technician receives a job card to replace an inspection panel on an engine pylon. The work requires climbing a ladder to access the panel. The aircraft is parked outside, and it is raining. Using the PEAR model, which category best fits the fact that this work must be done in the rain?

2. In the situation described in question 1, the ability of the technician to safely and efficiently climb a ladder and replace the panel best fits which category?

3. A technician working on aircraft interior repairs is approached by her supervisor and confronted with a mistake she made on a seat cover. The technician explains that the lighting at her station is inadequate to perform the work. The supervisor gladly submits a request to install additional lighting fixtures. Which human factors environment does the supervisor primarily represent?

4. A written document is needed to describe the knowledge, skills, and attitudes to perform the duty of maintenance technician at a regional airline. The supervisors decide to formulate a job task analysis (JTA) and use this document to assist in hiring, training, and promoting, employees. Is this a safe and workable strategy?

5. The "dirty dozen" is a list of 12 common human factors that affect the work place. An aircraft inspector decides not to look at an oil filter installation that a fellow employee has just accomplished. The employee has installed numerous filters previously and has always done the work correctly. Which of the dozen does this best describe?

HUMAN FACTORS

6. An airliner full of passengers is about to depart. The pilot notices a flashing red warning light on the instrument panel. Maintenance is called and directed to correct the problem immediately, or it will cost the airline thousands of dollars. The supervisor tells the technician to "extinguish the light, whatever it takes, and now", This is an example of what factor from the "dirty dozen"?

Section B
Exercises

1. What are some suggestions to help mitigate the problems caused by fatigue?

2. Technical documentation is a critical resource that can lead to what problems in aviation maintenance.

3. Explain the term norms as it pertains to aircraft maintenance.

4. What percentage of accidents are caused by human factors?

Section C
Final Chapter Exam - Multiple Choice

1. The study of organization psychology is concerned with the relationship between people and their work.
   ☐ A. True
   ☐ B. False
   ☐ C. Cannot be determined.

2. The study of the dimensions and abilities of the human body is called _____
   ☐ A. anthropology.
   ☐ B. anthropometrics.
   ☐ C. anthology.

3. Which of the following factors is included in the PEAR model _____
   ☐ A. actions of people.
   ☐ B. repair method.
   ☐ C. principles of aerodynamics.

4. Human error is defined as _____
   ☐ A. human lack of ability.
   ☐ B. human inaction with intended circumstances.
   ☐ C. human action with unintended consequences.

5. Active and latent errors differ primarily in that the active error is _____
   ☐ A. an obvious event.
   ☐ B. hidden.
   ☐ C. never detectable.

6. When two technicians are working on the same project, on different work shifts, a _____ is required to facilitate communication and provide safety.
   ☐ A. oral or written turnover
   ☐ B. job task analysis
   ☐ C. signature

7. Performing aircraft work without proper documentation may be a sign of _____
   ☐ A. efficiency.
   ☐ B. mitigating risk.
   ☐ C. complacency.

8. A technician installing a nose wheel tire is called away for a routine phone call. Upon returning to work, the technician forgets to torque the retaining bolts. This is an example of _____
   ☐ A. distraction.
   ☐ B. fatigue.
   ☐ C. pressure.

9. A defensive and rude supervisor is an unsafe supervisor because of the effect they may have upon _____
   ☐ A. fatigue and distraction.
   ☐ B. teamwork and communication.
   ☐ C. facilities and environment.

10. A composite repair to the tail of a modern aircraft, using materials on hand that are not approved for use on that aircraft, could be an example of _____
    ☐ A. lack of knowledge.
    ☐ B. lack of resources.
    ☐ C. both A and B.

Chapter 14, Final Chapter Exam - Human Factors

Name:_____ Date:_____

PAGE LEFT BLANK INTENTIONALLY

ANSWERS

CHAPTER 1
Safety, Ground Operations, and Servicing

Section A - Fill In The Blanks

1. Orderly, Clean
2. Technicians, Supervisors
3. Rubber Gloves, Safety Glasses, Grounded or Rubber Safety Mats.
4. Heat
5. Kinks, Bends
6. Tire Cage Guards
7. Safety Diamonds
8. Material Safety Data Sheets (MSDS)
9. Class A, Class B, and Class C
10. Fire Extinguishers
11. FOD
12. Level
13. Propeller Blast, Jet Exhaust
14. Propeller
15. Reciprocating

Section A - True or False

1. True
2. False
3. True
4. False
5. True
6. False
7. True
8. True
9. True
10. True
11. True
12. True
13. False
14. True
15. True

Section B - Fill In The Blanks

A. Stop
B. Come Ahead
C. Emergency Stop
D. Cut Engines
E. Start Engines
F. Pull Wheel Chocks
G. Place Wheel Chocks
H. Slow Down
I. All Clear
J. Left Turn
K. Right Turn
L. Night Operations

Section B - Short Answers

1. It makes them aware of how it affects maintenance performance. Several areas include fatigue, deadline pressure, stress, distractions, poor communication skills, complacency and lack of information.
2. Communicate with them, reminding them of their safety and that of others around them.
3. A working knowledge of the principles of electricity and a healthy respect for its capability to both work and damage. Wearing or use of proper safety equipment can provide psychological assurance and physically protect the user. Two factors that affect safety are fear and overconfidence.
4. Grinders are used to sharpen tools, dress metal, and perform other operations involving the removal of small amounts of metal. Precautions should be taken.
5. A knowledge of what causes a fire, how to prevent it, and how to put it out.

6. Oxygen, heat and fuel.
7. Water has two effects on fire. It deprives fire of oxygen and cools the material being burned.
8. Like water they deprive the fire of oxygen and cool the burning material.
9. As a general rule, only rated pilots and qualified A&P technicians are authorized to start, run up, and taxi aircraft. Many ground accidents have occurred as a result of improper technique in taxiing aircraft. A taxi signalman can assist the pilot or technician around the flight line.
10. Aircraft are to be tied down after each flight to prevent damage from sudden storms.

Section B - Exercises

1. Observe the rotor head and blades to see if they are level; this allows maximum clearance. Approach in view of the pilot. Never approach carrying anything with a vertical height that the blades could hit. Never approach a single-rotor helicopter from the rear or go from one side to the other by going around the tail. Always go around the nose.
2. Head the aircraft into the prevailing wind whenever possible. Chock all wheels, fore and aft. Attach tie down ropes, cables, or reels, forward and aft, to the appropriate ground anchors. Install control locks, all covers and guards.
3. A fireguard should stand by with a CO_2 fire extinguisher, clear of the propeller, while the aircraft engine is being started. They must be familiar with the induction and exhaust systems of the engine so that in case of fire, they can direct the CO_2 into the air intake or exhaust of the engine to extinguish it.
4. An aircraft parked in a hangar must be statically grounded. Chock all wheels, fore and aft. Attach tie down ropes, cables, or reels, forward and aft, to the appropriate ground anchors. Install control locks, all covers and guards.

CHAPTER 2
Regulations, Maintenance Forms, Records, and Publications

Section A - Multiple Choice

1. B
2. C
3. A
4. A
5. C
6. B
7. A
8. C
9. A
10. C
11. A
12. B
13. A
14. B
15. A
16. A
17. C
18. A
19. A
20. B

Section B - Short Answers

1. 43 Appendix B
2. 43.3
3. AC 43.13
4. 91.413
5. When performing a major repair or alteration.
6. Deficiencies or unsafe conditions in aircraft.
7. Specific descriptions and limitations.
8. Original equipment manufacturer (OEM).

ANSWERS

9. Special, experimental.
10. The applicable ASTM requirements.

Chapter 3
Mathematics in Aviation Maintenance

Section A - Multiple Choice
1. Tolerances, Fuel Calculations, Sheet Metal Repair

2. B	10. A	18. C	26. B
3. A	11. A	19. A	27. A
4. C	12. A	20. B	28. B
5. A	13. C	21. B	29. B
6. A	14. B	22. A	30. A
7. A	15. B	23. B	
8. C	16. A	24. A	
9. C	17. A	25. C	

Section B - Short Answers
1. No
2. 800 Miles
3. 160 Quarts
4. 20 psi
5. 675 Feet
6. 5/12 of the job
7. .004 inches or four thousandths.
8. 8:1
9. 20,736 Cubic Feet
10. .0076 Microfarads
11. 6944.44 or 6916.56 Cubic Yards of Asphalt
12. 254.66 Mile Trip
13. 678.58 Cubic Inch Displacement
14. No, 18.44 square feet are needed.
15. 75 Feet Tall

Chapter 4
Aircraft Drawings

Section A - Fill In The Blanks
1. Computer Graphics
2. Computer Aided Design Drafting
3. Computer Aided Engineering
4. Detailed, Assembly, Installation, Sectional View
5. Print
6. Drawing Number, Number of Part, Scale Name of Checker, Date, Firm Name, Name of Draftsman, Name of Person Approving Drawing
7. Perspective
8. Isometric View
9. Schematic
10. Flowcharts

Section A - True or False
1. False		4. True	
2. True		5. True	
3. False			

Section A - Matching
1. B	4. C	7. G	10. J
2. A	5. D	8. H	
3. E	6. F	9. I	

Section B - Short Answers
1. Drawing must provide information such as size and shape of the object and of all of its parts, specifications for material to be used, how the material is to be finished, how the parts are to be assembled, and any other information essential to making and assembling the particular object.
2. It is the allowable variation from the given dimension on the drawing. A + Figure indicates the maximum and a – indicates the minimum variation from the given dimension.
3. When parts or objects are much larger than the area available for the drawing it must be drawn to some scale. If it was small enough to fit on the drawing paper it could be drawn to a scale of 1:1. But if it is larger it must be drawn to scale, such as 1 inch on the drawing represents 1 foot on the object.
4. The exact location of the damage should be referenced by station, waterline and so forth. Using a measuring scale also will help determine the extent of the damage.

Section B - Exercises
1. No
2. Left and Right Engine Bleed Air.
3. Screw
4. 14-16 Gauge Wire.
5. 6.800 + or - .02 lbs per gal.
6. Figure Identification

A. Phantom Line	F. Break Line
B. Center Line	G. Dimension Line
C. Outline	H. Extension Line
D. Hidden Line	I. Sectioning Line
E. Cutting Plane Line	J. Leader Line

Chapter 5
Physics

Section A - Fill In The Blanks
1. Matter, Energy	6. Kinetic Energy
2. Matter	7. Force
3. Attraction	8. Force, Distance
4. Hydrometer, liquids	9. Rolling Friction
5. Potential energy	10. Time

Section A - True or False
1. True	6. True	11. True	16. False
2. False	7. True	12. True	17. True
3. True	8. True	13. False	18. True
4. False	9. False	14. True	19. False
5. False	10. True	15. True	20. True

Section A - Matching
1. Pure water boils:
   Celsius (A) ; Kelvin (E), Fahrenheit (D); Rankine (F).
   Pure water freezes: Celsius B; Kelvin (I), Fahrenheit (H); Rankine (G).
2. Molecular motion ceases at absolute zero:
   Celsius (C), Fahrenheit (J)

Section B - Matching

1. Flight Controls
   - A. Leading Edge Flaps
   - B. Leading Edge Slats
   - C. Flight Spoilers
   - D. Outboard Ailerons
   - E. Balance Tab
   - F. Outboard Flap
   - G. Inboard Aileron
   - H. Inboard Aileron
   - I. Inboard Flap
   - J. Ground Spoilers
   - K. Anti-Servo Tab
   - L. Elevator Tab
   - M. Elevator
   - N. Lower Rudder
   - O. Upper Rudder
   - P. Stabilizer

2. Wing Terminology
   - A. Cord Line
   - B. Upper Camber
   - C. Trailing Edge
   - D. Lower Camber
   - E. Relative Wind
   - F. Angle Of Attack

Section B - Short Answers

1. That due to position, that due to distortion of an elastic body, that which produces work through chemical action.
2. Weight and volume.
3. Force, distance, time.
4. A gauge that takes into account and includes atmospheric pressure in its reading along with the pressure its measuring.
5. Mach number has been given to the ratio of the speed of the aircraft to the speed of sound.
6. Temperature and pressure.
7. Thrust, drag, lift, weight.
8. Pressure decreases, velocity increases.
9. Pressure increases, velocity decreases.
10. Longitudinal, vertical, lateral.
11. The ailerons cause the airplane to move around the longitudinal axis or roll. The ailerons are attached to the trailing edge of the wings outboard that move opposite directions from each other. When one goes up the other goes down. This action causes the aircraft to roll in the direction of the up aileron. By reversing this action the aircraft will roll in the opposite direction.
12. The relative wind is the air flow opposite that of the aircraft.
13. The main rotor must produce enough lift to equal the weight of the aircraft. The engine must be producing enough power to drive the main rotor and antitorque system.
14. Autorotation is a flight condition where the main rotor blades are driven by the force of the relative wind pass through the blades, rather than by the engine.
15. It uses a hinged design that allows the rotor blade to flap up when it experiences increased lift and to flap down when it experiences decreased lift.

Section B - Exercises

1. Work = Force × Distance
   Work = 300 × 50
   Work = 15,000 ft lbs
2. Power = Force × Distance ÷ by Time
   Power = 550 lbs × 150 ft ÷ by 3 minutes
   Power = 27,500 ft lbs per minute
3. 27,500 ÷ by 33,000 = .83 HP
   The unit for 1 HP is 33,000 ft lbs per minute
4. Torque = 400 lbs × 5 inches
   Torque = 2,000 lb inch
5. Mechanical Advantage = Force Out ÷ by Force In
   E × 24 = 600 × 12
   E = 600 × 12 ÷ by 24
   E = 300
   600 lbs ÷ by 300 = 2
   Mechanical Advantage = 2 to 1

Chapter 6
Aircraft Weight and Balance

Section A - Fill In The Blanks, Multiple Choice, True or False

1. Safety, Efficiency
2. A
3. A
4. C
5. C
6. A
7. B
8. A
9. C
10. A
11. A
12. A
13. A
14. C
15. C
16. B
17. B
18. A
19. A
20. B
21. C
22. A
23. A
24. A
25. B
26. A
27. C
28. A
29. C
30. A

Section B - Short Answers

1. 210 pounds
2. Help
3. 84.94 inches aft of the datum.
4. 78.72 inches aft of the datum.
5. 34.46 inches aft of the datum.
6. Ballast added forward of the current CG.
7. Weight of the item and its location relative to the datum.
8. CG unchanged, aircraft now weighs 2686 pounds.
9. Cannot be determined..
10. Yes

Chapter 7
Aircraft Materials, Hardware, and Processes

Section A - Multiple Choice, True or False

1. A
2. C
3. B
4. A
5. A
6. A
7. B
8. A
9. C
10. A
11. C
12. B
13. A
14. A
15. B
16. C
17. A
18. A
19. B
20. C
21. A
22. C
23. C
24. A
25. B
26. B
27. A
28. C
29. C
30. A

Section B - Short Answers

1. Molybdenum 0.52%
2. None
3. Corrosion
4. 1,725 degrees °F
5. 1,600-1,700 degrees °F
6. 1,775-1,850
7. Water
8. Close Tolerance

ANSWERS

9. AN-350
10. Raised Cross

Chapter 8
Cleaning and Corrosion Control

Section A - Fill In The Blanks
1. AC 43-4A.-
2. Chemical, Electrochemical.
3. Surface, Internally.
4. Water, Water, Salt.
5. Corrosive.
6. Corrosion.
7. Chemical, Caustic, Gaseous.
8. Exhaust, Gaps, Seals, Hinges, Fairings.
9. Steel, Removal, Mechanical.
10. Dangerous.
11. Electrolytic.
12. Electrolytic Action.
13. Material Safety Data Sheets.
14. Methyl, Ethyl, Keytone, Acetone.
15. Kerosene.

Section A - True or False
1. True
2. False
3. True
4. True
5. False
6. True
7. False
8. True
9. False
10. False

Section A - Matching
1. Identify components from Figure.
   A. Current Flow
   B. Electron Flow
   C. Anodic Area
   D. Cathodic Area

2. Identify components from Figure.
   A. Cladding
   B. Anode
   C. Paint film
   D. Cathode
   E. Intergranualar Corrosion

3. Identify components from Figure.
   A. C
   B. B
   C. A
   D. G
   E. D
   F. F
   G. E
   H. H

Section B - Short Answers
1. Water or water vapor containing salt combines with oxygen in the atmosphere.
2. Direct chemical and electrochemical attack.
3. It is an attack resulting from a direct exposure of a bare surface to caustic liquid or gaseous agents.
4. It is similar to electrolytic reaction that takes place in electroplating, anodizing, or a dry cell battery. This attack requires a medium such as water to serve as an electrolyte.
5. Dissimilar metal corrosion.
6. The metal involved, its size and shape, its specific function, and atmospheric conditions.
7. A series of small worms under the painted surface.
8. The surface was improperly chemically treated

(prepared) prior to painting.
9. It occurs along the grain boundaries of an alloy and results from a lack of uniformity in the alloy structure. This is caused by changes in the heating and cooling of the material during manufacturing.
10. Climate, foreign material
11. Exhaust trail areas, battery compartments and vent openings, bilge areas, wheel well and landing gear areas. Water entrapment areas, engine frontal areas and cooling air vents, wing flap and spoiler recesses, external skin areas, hinges, control cables.
12. Cleaning and stripping, Removing corrosion, Neutralizing residual corrosion, Restoring protective surface films, Applying coatings or paint finishes
13. Use abrasive papers and compounds, small power buffers and buffing compounds, hand wire brush or steel wool.
14. A thin coating of relatively pure aluminum is applied over the base alloy. Pure aluminum has a high corrosive resistance.
15. Material Safety Data Sheet (MSDS).

Section B - Troubleshooting
1. Any metal surfaces that can contact a corrosive agent such as salt water (electrolyte) can start electrochemical attack on the metal. Areas that can hold water such as bilge wheel well or any water entrapment areas are very susceptible to corrosive attack.
2. First the hole should be opened up and the water completely drained from the aircraft. Then the area must be given a very close inspection for corrosion damage.
3. (1) Magnesium wheels, especially around bolt heads, lugs, and wheel web areas, particularly for the presence of entrapped water or its effects. (2) Exposed rigid tubing, especially at B-nuts and ferrules, under clamps and tubing identification tapes. (3) Exposed position indicator switches and other electrical equipment. (4) Crevices between stiffeners, ribs, and lower skin surfaces, which are typical water and debris traps.
4. Relieve the tension of the cables and check for internal corrosion. Replace cables that have internal corrosion. If the corrosion is limited to the external part of the cables, remove the corrosion and recoat with preservative.
5. It should be cleaned, treated, and painted as appropriate.

Section B - Exercises
1. No.
2. Aluminum wool, nylon webbing impregnated with aluminum oxide, abrasive fine grade non-woven abrasive pads or fiber bristle brushes.
3. Material Safety Data Sheet (MSDS).
4. Structural repair manual, dimensional tolerance limits, manufacturer.
5. At least 2 coats of zinc chromate or epoxy primer.

Chapter 9
Fluid Lines and Fittings

Section A - Fill In The Blanks
1. Outside diameter, sixteenths.
2. Accurate identification.
3. Excessive vibration, improper installation, damage.
4. Initial installation, pressure tested.
5. Metal tubing, flexible hose.
6. Square, burrs.
7. Fine tooth hacksaw.
8. 1/4-in., bending tool.
9. 10%.
10. Automotive type, 45 degrees.
11. Black, blue.
12. Pure rubber.
13. Neoprene.
14. Size.
15. Lay lines, printed.

Section A - True or False
1. True	5. True	9. True	13. True
2. False	6. True	10. False	14. False
3. True	7. True	11. True	15. True
4. False	8. False	12. False	

Section A - Matching
1. D	3. A
2. C	4. B

Section B - Short Answers
1. Cutting, bending, flaring, beading
2. Rotate toward the open side of the cutter.
3. Using a deburring tool sometimes attached to the cutting tool removes burred edges where the tube was cut.
4. Use care that the wall thickness at the end of the tubing is not reduced.
5. Cut tube squarely; remove burrs; slip fitting nut and sleeve on tubing; using a flaring tool, flare the end of the tube.
6. Scratches or nicks not deeper than 10% of the wall thickness in aluminum alloy tubing, which are not in the heel or bend.
7. Ensure that the layout of the new line is the same as the old line.
8. Buna-N, Neoprene, Butyl, Ethylene, Propylene, Dieve, Rubber, and Teflon.
9. Low, medium, and high pressure.
10. Lines, letters, and numbers.

Section B - Exercises
1. 60-85 inch lbs.
2. MS 21906
3. AN 815
4. Purple
5. 3 in. radii
6. Deterioration, leakage, separation of cove or braid from the inner tube, cracks, hardening, lack of flexibility and cold flow.
7. Proof-tested by applying pressure to the inside of the hose.
8. Answer Description:
   A. Place hose in vise and cut to desired length using fine tooth hacksaw or cut off wheel.
   B. Locate length of hose to be cut off and slit cover with knife to wire braid. After slitting cover, twist off with pair of pliers.
   C. Place hose in vise and screw socket on hose counterclockwise.
   D. Lubricate inside of hose and nipple threads liberally.
   E. Screw nipple into socket using wrench on hex of nipple and leave 0.005" to 0.031" clearance between nipple hex and socket.
9. Slack, flex, twisting, bending, clearance.
10. 5-8%, every 24 in., Identification stripe (lay line) does not spiral around the hose.

Chapter 10
Inspection Concepts and Techniques

Section A - Multiple Choice, True or False
1. A	6. A	11. C	16. C
2. C	7. B	12. B	17. A
3. B	8. A	13. B	18. A
4. B	9. A	14. C	19. C
5. C	10. A	15. C	20. A

Section B - Short Answers
1. Continuous.
2. Leakage.
3. IA, repair station, manufacturer.
4. 24 calendar months.
5. Severe.
6. Composite.
7. Corrosion, bent or broken parts.
8. Eddy current.
9. Living tissue must not be exposed.
10. Good penetration, uniform, free of pockets or inclusions.

Chapter 11
Hand Tools and Measuring Devices

Section A - Fill In The Blanks
1. Weight.
2. Surfaces, damaged.
3. Wood, brass, lead, rawhide, hard rubber, plastic.
4. Full face.
5. 75%.
6. Phillips, Reed & Prince.
7. Diagonal, Needlenose, Duckbill.
8. Length.
9. Center punch.
10. Box end.
11. Ratcheting box end wrench.
12. Crowfoot wrench.
13. Torque wrench.
14. Deflecting beam, dial indicating, micrometer, electronic setting.
15. Aluminum alloy, stainless steel.

ANSWERS

Section A - True or False

1. True	5. True	9. True	13. True
2. False	6. False	10. False	14. False
3. True	7. False	11. True	15. True
4. True	8. True	12. False	

Section B - Matching

A. Anvil
B. Measuring Faces
C. Spindle
D. Frame
E. Clamp Ring
F. Barrel
G. Thimble
H. Micrometer Screw
I. Fixed Nut
J. Thread Play Adjusting Nut
K. Thimble Cap
L. Ratchet Stop

Section B - Short Answers

1. Do not make pliers work beyond their capacity and do not use pliers to turn nuts because of damage.
2. Used for driving out damaged rivets, pins, bolts.
3. They must be tested (calibrated) at periodic intervals to ensure accuracy.
4. They are used for filing circular openings or concave surfaces.
5. The shank, the body and the heel.
6. 0.007.
7. Cut full threads to the bottom of a blind hole.
8. It is a tool that cuts a cone shaped depression around a rivet hole to allow the rivet to set flush with the surface material.
9. Fixed frame, barrel and anvil/movable thimble and spindle.
10. Inside, outside, depth.

Section B - Short Answers, Matching

1. Soft face.
2. Offset screwdriver.
3. Center punch.
4. Box end wrench.
5. Torque wrench.
6. Hacksaw, 32 teeth per inch.
7. 0.1285
8. Use the proper tap and clean out the threads.
9. #21
10. 5/16"
11. 873
12. (A) 0.1005; (B) 0.2154; (C) 0.2947; (D) 0.2944

Chapter 12
Fundamentals of Electricity and Electronics

Section A - Multiple Choice, True or False

1. A	9. C	17. B	25. B
2. C	10. A	18. C	26. A
3. A	11. C	19. B	27. B
4. A	12. C	20. A	28. A
5. C	13. A	21. A	29. C
6. B	14. A	22. A	30. A
7. C	15. B	23. B	
8. C	16. B	24. A	

Section B - Short Answers

1. Opposite, N to S.
2. 1 amp.
3. 80 volts.
4. 13.5 amps.
5. Battery, switch, fuse, wire, light.
6. 5.76 watts.
7. 21 ohms.
8. 24 volts.
9. 9.17 amps.
10. 48 volts.

Chapter 13
Mechanic Privileges and Limitations

Section A - Multiple Choice, True or False

1. C	6. B	11. A	16. C
2. A	7. C	12. B	17. A
3. B	8. B	13. A	18. A
4. A	9. A	14. B	19. B
5. C	10. C	15. A	20. A

Section B - Short Answers

1. 2 Years
2. Within 30 days.
3. Yes
4. None
5. No
6. No
7. Yes
8. Yes
9. Yes, on two accounts.
10. Yes

Chapter 14
Human Factors

Section A - Fill in the Blanks

1. Clinical Psychology, Experimental Psychology, Anthropometrics, Computer Science, Cognitive Science, Safety Engineering, Medical Science, Organizational Psychology, Educational Psychology, and Industrial Engineering
2. Human Factors
3. Experimental Psychology
4. People, Environment, Actions and Resources
5. Software (procedures), Hardware (machines), Environment (ambient) and Liveware (personnel).
6. Clinical Psychology
7. Experimental Psychology
8. Anthropometry
9. Safety Engineering
10. Cognitive Science
11. Organizational Psychology
12. Educational Psychology
13. Active error
14. Intentional error
15. Unintentional error

Section A - True or False
1. True	5. True	9. False	13. True
2. True	6. True	10. True	14. True
3. False	7. True	11. True	15. True
4. False	8. False	12. False	

Section B - Short Answers
1. Environment
2. People
3. Organizational
4. Yes
5. Complacency
6. Pressure

Section B - Exercises
1. They include looking for symptoms of fatigue in one's self and others. Have others check your work, even if an inspector sign off is not required. Avoid complex tasks during the bottom of your circadian rhythm. Sleep and exercise daily. Eight to nine hours of daily sleep are recommended to avoid fatigue.
2. When trying to find out more about the task at hand or how to troubleshoot and repair a system, often the information needed cannot be found because the manuals or diagrams are not available. If the information is not available, personnel should ask a supervisor or speak with a technical representative at the appropriate aircraft manufacturer.
3. Norms is short for "normal", or the way things are normally done. They are unwritten rules that are followed or tolerated by most organizations. Negative norms can detract from the established safety standard and cause an accident to occur. Norms are usually developed to solve problems that have ambiguous solutions.
4. Historically, twenty percent of all accidents are caused by a machine failure, and eighty percent of all accidents are caused by human factors.